Reality Check

NEIL T. ANDERSON
RICH MILLER

HARVEST HOUSE PUBLISHERS
Eugene, Oregon 97402

Cover by Garborg Design Works, Minneapolis, Minnesota

REALITY CHECK

ISBN 1-56507-409-2

Printed in the United States of America.

00 01 02 / BC / 10 9 8 7 6 5

THE 10–40 CHALLENGE!

We're always being told to "break this habit" or "kick that habit." But not all habits are bad. For example, brushing the mildew off your teeth every morning will help keep your breath from scorching the eyebrows off your friends. That's an example of a good habit.

Well, we've got a challenge for you. It's to develop a habit far more important than brushing your teeth—it's the awesome habit of meeting with God each day!

We call it the *10–40 Challenge!* What's that, you're wondering? Thought you'd never ask!

The challenge goes like this:

Take at least 10 minutes a day

for

40 days

. . . and then see if you haven't developed the greatest habit of all—spending daily time in the presence of your heavenly Father. He loves you and has incredible things to show you about Himself and your walk of faith in Him.

And guess what? *Reality Check* just happens to contain 40 short devotionals that can jump-start your day (or finish it off with a bang). Each devotional is designed so you can spend 10 minutes (or longer if you like) with Jesus to get your "spiritual tank" filled for the day ahead.

So while you're breaking the habit of eating 10 bowls of Sugar Bubbles cereal before bed, why not make a new habit and take the *10–40 Challenge!*

It's an invitation to the most exciting adventure this side of heaven—getting to know Almighty God in an up-close and personal way! If you want to take the challenge, then sign your name below!

I, ________________, hereby accept the

10–40 Challenge

to develop the awesome habit of

meeting daily with God.

Today's Date:____________.

Contents

Day 1

When in Doubt, Read the Owner's Manual!

Trust in the Lord with all your heart, and do not lean on your own understanding. In all your ways acknowledge Him, and He will make your paths straight (Proverbs 3:5,6).

"This job will take five minutes max," I proudly declared to myself as I prepared to change the right headlight on my minivan.

After a quick inspection, however, I realized it would not be as easy as I first expected to get at the old, burned-out lamp. But I had my trusty screwdriver in hand, and I could see exactly what needed to be done—so I thought!

"Well, maybe 15 minutes, but no more," I assured myself as I started to work eagerly on screw number one.

Thirty minutes later, after much perspiration, a cut hand, and several choice words, I was no closer to finishing the job than when I had begun. Then I remembered the wise words of my dad, spoken to me years before: "Son, when in doubt, read the owner's manual!"

"Oh, yeah," I groaned, "the owner's manual." Feeling a little stupid, I swallowed my pride, admitted I didn't know what to do, and got out the manual.

It turns out I was right after all: It *was* a five-minute job—once I found out from the owner's manual how to do it right!

It's so easy for us to get faked out by our own pride. We burst on a new situation in life with great confidence, our minds quickly assess the facts of the case, and we plunge ahead with our own solution, certain that our success is assured.

But that is not God's way. We must learn to trust our owner (God) and His Manual for our lives (the Bible). You see, life is far more complex than a minivan. God understands completely what is going on, but we don't. He knows the right way to think, feel, and act in any and every situation, but we don't. He knows all the pitfalls that lie in the road ahead, but we don't.

When we foolishly "lean on our own understanding," we one day find that we have been building our lives on a faulty foundation. We are like a crippled man leaning on crutches made from rotting wood: A painful, humbling fall is inevitable.

In fact, the Bible promises that pride will lead to big-time trouble. Proverbs 16:18 warns that "pride goes before destruction, and a haughty spirit before stumbling."

Do you have a good, sharp mind? Do you have the ability to think and act quickly and decisively? If so, praise God for it, since He is the One who has given you this mind. Why not begin to let God fill your mind with His truth and wisdom for life by reading and meditating on His Word?

Trust in the Lord with *all* your heart. He will guide you in every decision of life. In every area of your life, acknowledge that you need Him. Then He will make your paths straight.

When in doubt, read the Owner's Manual—the Word of God!

Reality Check

In what areas of your life do you tend to rely on yourself instead of trusting in God and His wisdom?

God knows you inside out. He loves you and is committed to making your life the best it can be. And He has all the power in the universe at His command to carry out His plans for you. How does knowing these things help you to rely on God rather than on yourself?

Think of a recent example when you trusted God for something and it worked out smoothly. Think of another recent example when you took matters into your own hands and things got messed up.

Look up the following verses in your Bible. In the blanks provided, summarize what they say about trusting God and His Word as opposed to trusting in yourself and your own abilities.

Proverbs 28:25,26

Isaiah 40:28-31

The Lie to Reject

I reject the lie that says I am able, by myself, to figure out how to live life and solve my problems. I reject the lie of my pride that tells me this is the "strong way to live."

The Truth to Accept

I accept the truth that apart from Jesus I can do nothing (John 15:5), *but that I can do all things through Him who strengthens me* (Philippians 4:13).

Prayer for Today

Lord, thank You for showing me how strong and wise and loving You are. Thank You for showing me how weak I am without You. You are my life and I choose today to trust in You with all my heart. I choose to allow You through Your Word and Your Spirit to guide and direct me. I don't want to rely on myself. Please remind me, whenever I have a decision or choice to make, to ask You for guidance. I thank You for Your promise to make my paths straight because You delight to show me Your ways. In Jesus' name. Amen.

Today's Bible Reading: John 1

Further Reading: Psalm 37 and John 15

Day 2

No Cuts from God's Team

You are a chosen race, a royal priesthood, a holy nation, a people for God's own possession, that you may proclaim the excellencies of Him who has called you out of darkness into His marvelous light (1 Peter 2:9 NASB).

As a lowly sophomore in high school, baseball was everything to me. It was my ticket from low man on the totem pole to somebody important. And the varsity baseball coach was like a god to me.

I felt like he held my happiness in his calloused hands, for he had the power to cut me from the squad or put my name on that treasured list called "the team."

I knew from my older brother that the coach was moody, quick-tempered, and unpredictable. If he liked you, you were in; if not, forget it. And so I was afraid of him.

During tryouts I worked as hard as I could—at least as hard as my six-foot-two-inch, 140-pound body would let me. I wanted so much to please the coach and make the team. I didn't care if I warmed the junior varsity bench, gathering splinters in my posterior. I just wanted to put on that uniform and know I belonged.

One cold and gray March afternoon I lost my cool. We had been doing the same drill for nearly two hours, and my hands were almost frozen. So I asked the coach sarcastically, "Are we going to do this same thing all day?"

Wrong thing to say to a coach! He gave me a stare that froze the rest of my body.

The next day at practice he ambled up to me and said, "We've got 17 guys trying out for pitcher here. You don't have to worry about coming to practice anymore." And then he turned and walked away.

And that was it. My dream was over, and I felt like my hopes for making it in high school were shattered. You could have scraped my self-image off the ground, I felt so low.

I tried to get back on the coach's good side by becoming manager of the team, but it didn't work. To him I was a nobody.

Sometimes we can be afraid of our heavenly Father. We walk on eggshells, afraid that we'll do the wrong thing and that will be it. We fear He will turn His back on us and walk away disgusted.

But there are no cuts from God's team! As 1 Peter 2:9 declares, He has chosen us, given us a royal position in His family, made us holy, and called us to Himself. We belong to Him!

When we stand before Christ and the books are opened, all who have trusted in Jesus alone to save them from sin will have their names on God's "list"—the Lamb's book of life.

So take a deep breath and let out a big sigh of relief: "There is therefore now no condemnation for those who are in Christ Jesus" (Romans 8:1). Jesus is with us even to the end of the age (Matthew 28:20), and God will never leave us or forsake us (Hebrews 13:5).

God loves us in Christ whether we're good, bad, or

ugly. *Nothing* can separate us from the love that God has for us through Jesus Christ! Now that's something to get excited about.

In fact, that's what God tells us to do: "Proclaim the excellencies of Him who has called you out of darkness into His marvelous light." Why not tell someone today what great things God has done for you!

Reality Check

Do you find it hard or easy to believe that God completely accepts you as you are through faith in Jesus? Why?

When you mess up and then feel ashamed or guilty for what you have done, what should you do? (See 1 John 1:7-9).

Some people think that if God loves Christians even when they sin, this will motivate people to take advantage of His love. Do you agree or disagree with that opinion? Why or why not?

Look up the following verses in your Bible. In the blanks provided, summarize what they say about what our attitude should be toward coming into God's presence.

Hebrews 4:14-16

Hebrews 10:19-22

The Lie to Reject

I reject the lie of Satan that my heavenly Father is in any way cruel, moody, easily angered, rejecting, or condemning. I reject all of the devil's slanderous lies about God that would cause me to be afraid of Him.

The Truth to Accept

I accept the truth that my heavenly Father loves me and that I am not just "on His team" but am part of His family! He will never reject or condemn me in Christ. I am His precious child and He is pleased with me because of what Christ has done for me.

Prayer for Today

Lord, I thank You so much that You love me just the way I am in Christ. You have totally accepted me, and I don't have to be afraid anymore that You will one day give up on me. Although not everything I do pleases You, I know that You are pleased with me as a person. Strengthen me today to walk in these truths, not taking advantage of Your wonderful love, but expressing my love back to You in obedience and praise. In Jesus name. Amen.

Today's Bible Reading: John 2

Further Reading: Psalm 103 and Romans 8

Day 3

Who in the World Am I?

As many as received Him [Jesus], to them He gave the right to become children of God, even to those who believe in His name (John 1:12).

Jason (not his real name) looked confused and afraid. He was holding one side of his face as he sat quietly near the front of the noisy auditorium.

Minutes earlier he had given public testimony of his new faith in Christ and had even confessed to the group an act of vandalism he had committed the night before. As a result of Jason's humble stand for Christ, many other students had come forward to find forgiveness and freedom in Jesus. I had walked over to thank him for his courage when I saw his distress.

Jason told me that one whole side of his face was going numb, almost as if Novocain had been shot into his cheek. He was finding it increasingly hard to talk.

"Have you ever had this happen before?" I asked.

"Just once," he replied. "Last night when I received Christ."

I suspected that a spiritual battle was taking place for this young man, and so I invited him to come upstairs where we could talk privately. As we sat at the table in the camp cafeteria, Jason continued to get worse.

Not knowing how to help him, I prayed for his healing and for wisdom for myself. Then the idea came to me to have him read through a list of biblical statements about who we are in Christ.

As he started reading, he was struck by an excruciating pain in his neck and shoulder. It was crystal-clear to me by then that Jason was being cruelly attacked by the powers of darkness.

I exercised my authority in Christ over the enemy and Jason's pain eased enough for him to talk. He looked at me sadly and said, "Rich, not many people know this, but I'm an alcoholic."

"Jason, you are *not* an alcoholic. You are a child of God who has struggled with alcohol. There is a big difference." He nodded his head in agreement and out loud confessed his misuse of alcohol, declaring his commitment to give it up.

The horrible pain gripped him again as much as before. As I prayed for him I was wondering, What is going on here?

Then Jason turned to me again, and admitted, "Rich, I've never told anyone this before, but I'm a junkie."

I knew he needed to hear the truth again. "Jason, you are *not* a junkie. You are a child of God who has struggled with drugs!"

And so, one by one he confessed and renounced his use of five or six different drugs. Immediately the numbness left his face, and the terrible pain in his neck and shoulders disappeared. His face was nearly exploding with joy.

"You know, Rich," Jason beamed, "you would not believe the high that I get from crack..."

I was puzzled for a moment as to why he wanted me to know that, but then he continued:

". . . but *this* is so much better!"

What was the "this" Jason was talking about? *Freedom.* Freedom from the numbness and pain, to be sure, but it was more than that. It was freedom from guilt and shame and from having to wear the label "alcoholic" or "junkie."

Jason, one day old in Jesus, had learned a crucial truth: *Who we really are is who God says we are.* And God says that those who have trusted in Jesus are His *children.*

What label are you wearing today? Jock, nerd, partyer, brain, loner, no-good, worthless, loser, druggie, A.D.D., stud, and so on? You may hate the label that others have put on you or you may think it's kind of cool. You may have grown used to using your label as a way to keep people from expecting too much from you.

Don't you think it's about time to listen to God instead? He knows who you are, and He calls you His child.

Reality Check

How does it make you feel to know that God is your Father and you are His kid? What are some of the things your Father in heaven will do for you because you are His child?

If you are a Christian, you were once a sinner who was saved by the grace of God through faith in Jesus. But now you are a saint (holy one) who still happens to sin. Why is it so important to see yourself as a *saint* as opposed to a *sinner?*

What are some of the labels you have put on other people? How would seeing others the way God sees them change the way you treat those people?

Look up the following verses in your Bible. In the blanks provided, summarize what they say about who you are in Christ.

Romans 6:11-14

Romans 8:31-39

The Lie to Reject

I reject the lie that I am _______ (put in the incorrect labels). *I choose to no longer live by the world's standard that says "you are what you do." I reject any definition and description of myself that does not come from God and His Word.*

The Truth to Accept

I accept the truth that I am a child of God and a new creation in Christ. I declare that I am a saint, a holy one, and not a sinner anymore. Even though I still sin, God sees me as I truly am: completely cleansed and forgiven, accepted and set free to walk in newness of life in Christ.

Prayer for Today

Lord, You are the King and Ruler of all heaven and earth. Yet I can call You Father because I belong to You. Thank You that nothing can ever separate me from Your awesome love. Thank You that in Christ I am dead to sin and alive to God, so today I choose to walk in the newness of life in Christ. No matter what name or label others may call me, I rest in the assurance that You know who I am—Your child. Because of who Jesus is and what He has done, I pray these things. Amen.

Today's Bible Reading: John 3

Further Reading: 1 Corinthians 1 and Ephesians 1

Day 4

Face-to-Face with a Murderer

As those who have been chosen of God, holy and beloved, put on a heart of compassion, kindness, humility, gentleness and patience; bearing with one another, and forgiving each other, whoever has a complaint against anyone; just as the Lord forgave you, so also should you (Colossians 3:12,13).

Tom walked into the prison cell and looked into the face of the man who had murdered his older brother in cold blood.

The man, depressed and weary, confessed that all he wanted to do was to find a priest to pray with him so he could die. Instead, Tom and his friend brought him life: They shared the good news of Jesus Christ and His forgiveness.[1] After a fierce battle with the powers of darkness (the man had been heavily into the occult), the man knew he needed and wanted the Lord; he was able to cry out, "Jesus . . . save me!"

Instantly the man's stiff and convulsing body went limp and his agonized face grew soft. Christ had saved him and set him free! Realizing what had happened, this new brother in the Lord leaped to his feet and began dancing and clapping his hands like a little child. He praised God and told the evil spirits to "beat it" in the name of Jesus.

As the two men started to bid him farewell, the new believer asked for their names. The military officer introduced himself, then the man with him, Tom Roxas.

"Roxas?!" The man gasped at the familiar family name, reeling back.

"Yes, he's the brother of the man you killed," Tom's friend confirmed.

Suddenly the prisoner fell to the ground, his face to Tom's feet, sobbing, "Forgive me, forgive me!"

Tom knelt, lifted him up, and hugged him, saying, "Christ has forgiven me, and I also have forgiven you." In a rush of emotion they hugged, sobbed for joy, and praised God.

Days later, Tom and his friend visited their new brother to assure him again of his salvation. "I couldn't look into your eyes previously," the man confessed. "If I were in your place my blood would boil. Christ surely must be in you, for no man could forgive me as you have."

The new believer went on to assure Tom and his friend that he knew that the same Christ lived in him. He had already joyfully shared the good news of hope and forgiveness with another cellmate![2]

An incredible story: A guilty murderer is pardoned for eternity by the Judge, Jesus Christ. A prisoner behind bars is set free forever! A man, Tom Roxas, deeply hurt, grieved and angry over the senseless death of his brother, finds his heart overwhelmed with compassion for a cold-blooded killer. And he forgives him.

How is this possible? Only through the power of the One who cried out on the cross, "Father, forgive them, for they do not know what they are doing" (Luke 23:34).

The sad truth, however, is that all too many of God's children are not in jail but *are* in prison. Teenagers are behind bars in a prison of their own anger. Young men and women are shackled with the chains of bitterness and unforgiveness. Maybe I'm describing your life today.

Make the choice right now to let go of the complaints you have against those who have hurt you. Why spend another moment in prison when you can be free?

Let the compassion, kindness, humility, gentleness, and patience of the Crucified One wash over your soul. And forgive as Tom forgave that murderer. Forgive as Jesus forgave you.

Reality Check

Why is it sometimes so hard to forgive those who have hurt us? Because they

Jesus cried out on the cross, "It is finished!" He was declaring that the penalty for all sin for all time was paid in full. Based on that truth, why is harboring hatred and taking revenge against another person wrong?

Because Jesus forgave us, and them, for everything. It is over all of the trials should be done.

Ask the Lord to reveal to your mind all the people you need to forgive. Write their names on a piece of paper. Take some time today to forgive each and every one of them. Stick with each person on your list until you cannot recall anything else he or she has done to hurt you. The following prayer may help you in this crucial process:

Lord, I choose to forgive (name of person) *for* (what the person did to hurt you) *even though it made me feel* (share with God the emotional pain).

Look up the following verses in your Bible. In the blanks provided, summarize what they say about the importance of forgiveness.

Ephesians 4:31,32

we should forgive others, have compassion, get rid of bitterness, and turn it into forgiveness like Jesus did for us.

Matthew 6:9-15

Telling us that we must forgive people who hurt us as Jesus did.

The Lie to Reject

I reject the lie that says I have to pay back people for hurting me by taking revenge, hurting their reputation, or harboring anger inside. I reject the lie that says I have to hold on to my anger and hatred to protect myself from further hurt.

The Truth to Accept

I accept the truth that it is God's business and not mine to deal with those who have hurt me. He will act in perfect justice and mercy, something I cannot do. I accept the truth that forgiving others from my heart is the only path to freedom and healing for me.

Prayer for Today

Lord, I thank You that Christ has forgiven me of all my sins, even when I did not deserve it. In the same way, I choose to forgive those who have hurt me. I let go of all my anger and hatred, and I release these people into Your hands. I choose to walk in freedom, and I turn my back on all my bitter bondage. And now I ask you, Lord, to heal all the hurts in my heart. I know that it will take some time, but I choose to trust in You and let You protect me from this day forward.

In Jesus's name. Amen.

Today's Bible Reading: John 4

Further Reading: Genesis 37–50. This is a long passage of Scripture, but it is one of the most moving, powerful dramas in all of the Bible.

Day 5

Today Is the Day

Today if you hear His voice, do not harden your hearts (Hebrews 4:7).

In the movie *City Slickers,* Billy Crystal plays a dad who at one point goes into his son's school to talk about what he does for a living. All of a sudden he breaks into his analysis of life. It is not only funny, but filled with a reality that we all need to face:

> *Value this time in your life, kids, because this is the time in your life when you still have your choices. It goes by so fast.*
>
> *When you're a teenager, you think you can do anything and you do. Your twenties are a blur.*
>
> *Thirties, you raise your family, you make a little money, and you think to yourself, "What happened to my twenties?"*
>
> *Forties, you grow a little pot belly, you grow another chin. The music starts to get too loud, one of your old girlfriends from high school becomes a grandmother.*
>
> *Fifties, you have minor surgery—you'll call it a procedure, but it's surgery.*
>
> *Sixties, you'll have a major surgery, the music is*

still loud, but it doesn't matter because you can't hear it anyway.

Seventies, you and the wife retire to Fort Lauderdale. You start eating dinner at 2:00 in the afternoon, you have lunch around 10:00, breakfast the night before, spend most of your time wandering around malls looking for the ultimate soft yogurt and muttering, "How come the kids don't call? How come the kids don't call?"

The eighties, you'll have a major stroke, and you end up babbling with some Jamaican nurse who your wife can't stand, but who you call mama.

Any questions?[1]

An exaggeration? Sure. Too stereotyped? Probably. But two things from that quote ought to grab you by the collar and scream into your ears:

> *This is the time in your life when you still have your choices.*
>
> *When you're a teenager, you think you can do anything.*

God says, "*Today* if you hear His voice, do not harden your hearts." Today you have a choice; tomorrow you may not.

It's easy when you're young to blow off following God, thinking you've got all the time in the world. But God says, "*Today...*"

It's easy when you're feeling the excitement of your teenage years to want to do everything the world has to offer. And you want to do it now. God says, "*Today...*"

It's easy to think that God's voice will always call as loud and clear as it does at this point in your life. And so you tune to another "station." But God says, "*Today* . . ."

You see, there are only two choices: Open your heart or harden your heart. If you open your heart to what God is saying to you today, then you will continue to hear Him tomorrow. But each time you harden your heart, His voice grows a little fainter.

The warning that trumpets from the throne of God is:

> *Remember your Creator in the days of your youth, before the days of trouble come* (Ecclesiastes 12:1 NIV).

What has God been saying to you? *Today* make the choice not to harden your heart, but to open your heart.

Reality Check

Think about the areas in which you experience the severest temptation. How has Satan been trying to persuade you to ignore what God says and do what the non-Christian world says is okay?

Take a moment and ask the Lord to show you what He wants to say to you today. Write it down. Include any Bible verses that come to mind. Commit yourself before God today to open your heart rather than harden your heart.

Can you think of another brother or sister in Christ who

has been struggling in his or her relationship with God? Ask the Lord to show you today how you can encourage that person to open his or her heart to God.

Look up the following verses in your Bible. In the blanks provided, summarize what they say about hearing and doing the will of God.

James 1:22-27

To not just hear the word of God, but follow through with it also. To not ignore what you were called to do.

Psalm 85:8

The Lie to Reject

I reject the lie that tells me I have total control of my life and that I don't have to worry about seriously following God today. I reject the lie that says my choice to ignore God's voice today will have no effect on my future.

The Truth to Accept

I accept the truth that says what I do today does affect my future, both here on earth and in heaven. God says that "Today" is important, and so I choose today to open my heart to God and not harden my heart, no matter what He might show me.

Prayer for Today

Lord, thank You for showing me that I cannot play games with You and win. You are a holy God and Your Word is truth. Even though I am young, I am not invincible and You alone have the final say in my life. Today is the first day of the rest of my life, but it could also be the last. The only guarantee I have is that You love me and that You are in control. So I commit myself to following You. Please open my ears and eyes to hear You and see You at work in my life today. I want my heart to be wide open to all that You have for me. In Jesus' name. Amen.

Today's Bible Reading: John 5

Further Reading: Psalm 90 and James 4

Day 6

Selling Out

Jesus said to His disciples, "If anyone wishes to come after Me, let him deny himself, and take up his cross, and follow Me. For whoever wishes to save his life shall lose it; but whoever loses his life for My sake shall find it" (Matthew 16:24,25).

I rushed into the photographer's room irritated and impatient. It was a warm spring day and I wasn't too thrilled about wasting part of my day getting my college yearbook picture taken. Knowing that it was a "waist-up" picture, I was decked out in a dress shirt, tie, sports jacket (borrowed), shorts, and tennis shoes.

I wanted to get this business taken care of as soon as possible, and I let the photographer know how I felt.

But the man was a pro. He was a friendly, backslapping kind of guy who put me at ease right away with a few jokes. Pretty soon I was enjoying the time, even as he adjusted the lights, background, and camera angle.

When it was time to snap the pictures, the photographer asked me to say a profanity. I wondered, "Whatever happened to 'Cheese'!" But not wanting to make a scene, I went along with him.

I must have smiled when I said those words because the photographer seemed happy with the shots.

Glad to be done, I got up from the stool and started to leave. But the photographer stopped me and looked me straight in the eye.

"Y'know, Rich," he announced, grinning ear-to-ear, "you're a man after my own heart. The last person in here didn't want to say (the profanity). He wanted to say 'Jesus.' "

I felt as if a knife had gone straight into my heart. I grunted something to the photographer, smiled weakly, and bolted out of there as fast as I could.[1]

I knew I had sold out to sin, and I felt like dirt. Yeah, I was a Christian all right, but I had not been very serious about my faith . . . until that moment.

"Why had it been so important to me for that stupid photographer to like me?" I asked myself over and over again.

The answer is clear to me now: I wasn't willing to pay the price for my faith. I wanted everything to be easy. I wanted everyone to like me, and so I compromised my faith in Christ.

I had been far more concerned about pleasing people than pleasing God. I had not been willing to deny myself, take up my cross, and follow Christ.

God used that gut-wrenching incident to wake me up and shake me up. From that moment on I vowed that I would never deny Christ like that again.

And that's really the choice we all have to make: Deny self or deny Christ. Sell out to sin and the world's approval or sell out to Jesus. We cannot have both worlds.

Jesus put it this way: "No one can serve two masters" (Matthew 6:24). There are no exceptions to this rule. Not you and not me.

I wish I could go back and tell that photographer how I feel about Jesus now, but I can't. But I *can* choose today to deny myself, take up my cross, and follow Jesus . . . going where He tells me to go, doing what He tells me to do, saying what He tells me to say.

Maybe you have been selling out to the world, longing for the approval of people more than the approval of God. No, you can't change the past, but you can change *today*.

Joshua put it bluntly: "Choose for yourselves this day whom you will serve." I hope your answer will be like his: "But as for me and my household, we will serve the Lord" (Joshua 24:15 NIV).

REALITY CHECK

"Denying self"—giving up your own self-centered plans, goals, habits, attitudes, and actions—may be the hardest thing in the world to do. Yet Jesus says it is necessary in order to follow Him.

Why is denying self so key to following Christ?

Because we have flaws, and will be held back.

Why do we so often feel that it is more important to our happiness to please people than to please God?

Because people are here and we can see them, but we can't see God

What are some truths about God's character that help us to truly "sell out" to Him?

Look up the following verses in your Bible. In the blanks provided, summarize what they say about surrendering your life to follow Christ.

Luke 9:21-27

That we will be denied many things. We should deny ourselves everyday and take up our cross and follow him. That we have to lose our life to save it. That we can have the whole world but not have God.

Luke 9:57-62

We cannot look back and go back to do things before you follow Jesus, those things don't matter you must follow him w/out looking back.

The Lie to Reject

I reject the lie that says my happiness comes from doing what I want as opposed to what God wants. I reject the lie that tells me it is more important to be popular with my peers than it is to please God.

The Truth to Accept

I accept the truth that joy and peace are the result of walking by the Spirit's power **(Galatians 5:22,23)** ***and that true happiness comes from holiness*** **(Hebrews 1:9)*.***

I choose to believe the truth that when I please God I will not please all the people, but I will please the right *people.*

PRAYER FOR TODAY

Lord, I thank You that You made the tough choice to take up the cross and die for me. I thank You that You showed me the way to live by praying, "Father, not My will, but Yours be done." Please strengthen me today to deny myself, take up my cross and follow You. I desire today to go where You want me to go, do what You want me to do, and say what You want me to say, regardless of what people think. And help me to do it all in Your love. In Jesus' name. Amen.

TODAY'S BIBLE READING: JOHN 6

FURTHER READING: Acts 4 and Galatians 1

Day 7

It's True! . . . Believe It or Not!

Count yourselves dead to sin but alive to God in Christ Jesus. Therefore do not let sin reign in your mortal body so that you obey its evil desire (Romans 6:11,12 NIV).

"So, how long have you been dead?" the psychiatrist asked his relaxed patient. The man was lying peacefully on the office couch, his hands resting comfortably behind his head.

"Oh, for a long time now," the man calmly replied.

"I see. So what brings you into my office today? You seem to be quite content being dead. How can I help you?" The doctor could barely keep a straight face as he talked with him.

"Well, it's everybody else. I'm having a terrible time trying to convince other people that I'm dead. No one seems to want to believe me."

"That's understandable, Mr. Harris. After all, you can walk, talk, breathe, see, hear, and feel. These are things that dead people simply cannot do." The psychiatrist had decided to use a logical approach, all the while suspecting it was a lost cause.

"So, the truth comes out!" The patient rose angrily from his couch and pointed an accusing finger at the doctor. "You're like all the rest of them. You don't believe I'm dead either, do you?"

"No, Mr. Harris, I don't."

The patient started to stomp out the door in disgust when a brilliant idea hit the psychiatrist.

"Wait, Mr. Harris! Before you leave, could I ask you one simple question?" The doctor knew he had only one more chance to convince this obviously confused and disturbed young man that he was actually alive and well.

"All right. But this better be quick!"

"It will be, I assure you. Here's my question: Mr. Harris, do you believe that dead men bleed?"

"Doctor, that is the stupidest question I've ever heard. 'Do I believe that dead men bleed?' Of course dead men don't bleed. Everybody knows that!"

The wily psychiatrist had slowly maneuvered himself around to one of the drawers in his office and had secretly pulled out a syringe. With lightning speed he whirled around and plunged the needle deep into the man's shoulder.

"Yeow!" the patient yelled. "What are you doing? Are you some kind of a nut case?"

The grinning doctor placed himself between Mr. Harris and the door, waiting for the evidence to show.

"There! Do you see it, Mr. Harris? Look at your shoulder. It's bleeding! It's bleeding! Do you know what that means?" The gleeful psychiatrist was nearly jumping up and down, certain that his patient's healing was moments away.

"Well, I'll be darned," the shocked man exclaimed; "dead men do bleed after all!"

What a frustrating type of person to deal with! He's a living example of the "I've already made up my mind. Don't confuse me with the facts" kind of thinking.

How many Christian young people live the same way? They're convinced that they're stuck in sin, with no chance of ever escaping into freedom, when all along God says, "Consider yourselves to be dead to sin but alive to God in Christ Jesus."

How can we "consider ourselves to be dead to sin"? Because we are! Those are the facts. When Christ died on the cross and rose from the dead, the Bible says that we died and rose with Him (see Romans 6:1-11)!

At the moment we trusted Christ to save us, sin ceased being your master and my master. We now belong to God.

"Our old self [that sin-enslaved person] was crucified" with Jesus, so that "we should no longer be slaves to sin" (Romans 6:6).

The meaning of this verse is earthshaking, for a slave to sin has no choice but to sin, but *a free man can choose whom he or she will obey.*

Think of the toughest area of temptation and sin that you battle. Is it drugs? Alcohol? Sex? Anger? Rebellion? Unforgiveness? Depression? Anxiety? Fear? Guilt? No matter what it is, God's Word says you are free! You don't have to give in to that sin anymore. You are now free to choose righteousness.

Maybe you don't "feel" like Christ has set you free. Well, neither did the man in the story "feel" alive! Your feelings don't change for one second the facts of what God says is true!

So count yourself dead to sin and alive to God today. Sin is no longer your master, God is. It's true... believe it or not!

Reality Check

What does it mean to be a "slave to sin"? What does it mean to be a slave to God?

Means that you obey to sin, you do sin, w/out thinking, and you are not caring.

- means you follow god and are compassionate

To what area(s) of sin has Satan convinced you that you are still a slave? How does knowing the truth of this lesson help set you free?

- Helps by providing clarity, knowing that its not whats important, but following God is.

Being "dead to sin and alive to God" obviously does not mean that we can no longer sin. We can and still do sin. It means *we are now free to choose to obey God.* What are some of the lies the devil uses to try to persuade you to hang onto sin even though you don't have to?

Look up the following verses in your Bible. In the blanks provided, summarize what they say about the freedom we have to say no to sin and yes to God.

Titus 2:11-14

That the word of God teaches us to say No to sin, and says yes to self-controlled, upright, and godly lives. That God gave himself so we wouldnt have to be wicked, so we could purify ourselves and be good.

1 Peter 4:1-5

That God suffered so there wouldnt be any sin. ~~that~~ we should live for God not sin.

people who live evil ways and tempt you will one day be judged by God

The Lie to Reject

I reject the lie that says I am still a slave to sin. Although I may have been living as if that were true, I recognize it for what it is: a bald-faced lie of the devil designed to make me feel helpless and hopeless and get me to settle for less than what God says is true.

The Truth to Accept

I accept the truth (regardless of what my feelings say) that I am now dead to sin and alive to God in Christ Jesus. I therefore choose today to live according to that truth, and I refuse to obey sin's evil desires. I choose to obey God.

Prayer for Today

Lord, please forgive me for listening to what the devil says and what my feelings say rather than what You say is true in Your Word. I thank You that You have already set me free from my slavery to sin. I rejoice that when I trusted Jesus as Savior, Christ's victory over sin became a reality for me. When He died to sin on the cross, I died with Him. When He rose from the dead, I rose with Him to walk in the newness of life. Thank You, Lord, for assuring me that Your power is greater than the strongest temptation, and so I choose to walk with You today in the power of the Holy Spirit. In Jesus' name. Amen.

Today's Bible Reading: John 7

Further Reading: Romans 5 and 6

Day 8

Tools for Good or Weapons for Evil?

Do not offer the parts of your body to sin, as instruments of wickedness, but rather offer yourselves to God, as those who have been brought from death to life; and offer the parts of your body to him as instruments of righteousness (Romans 6:13 NIV).

What you do with your body really matters. This truth has powerfully hit home with me recently as I have talked with the following hurting people:

Stuart had lost control. He would spend endless hours in front of the tube, magnetically drawn to sexually arousing images. Though he knew it was wrong, he was engaging in sexual fantasies involving his girlfriend, and they had been involved physically beyond what God permitted. Stu was feeling guilt and shame.

Melinda was going nowhere fast spiritually. Perhaps in part as an effort to get back at a controlling mother, she had become sexually active. By the time I met her she was wrung out emotionally. She had gotten pregnant, had had an abortion and felt like she should be punished for the rest of her life for what she had done. Melinda was also feeling guilt and shame.

Randall was fighting a losing battle with sexual thoughts that clung to his mind like ticks to a dog. He had experimented with group masturbation as a boy and was now waking up in the middle of the night feeling helplessly trapped in that behavior. He had engaged in oral sex with his girlfriend and felt horrible about it. Guilt and shame were Randall's constant companions as well.

Three different young people with a lot in common—the most significant being that they all knew Christ personally.

No, this was not a trio of disgusting, wicked, heathen, pagan sinners. These were two brothers and a sister in the Lord who had fallen prey to sexual sin. Maybe you can relate.

But they had at least two other things in common as well. First, their sexual sin had shackled them in spiritual chains so that they were not experiencing their freedom in Christ. Second, all three left the counseling session rejoicing that Jesus had set them free!

What had been their downfall? *Offering the parts of their bodies to sexual sin rather than offering them to God for good.* And the result was that they forfeited their freedom in Christ and fell into the cesspool of guilt and shame.

Sure, they had experienced a measure of pleasure for a short while, but was it worth it in the end? If it *was* worth it, why did they cry out for help? Why did they confess and renounce every sexual use of their bodies as instruments of unrighteousness?

Because in the long run, it *wasn't* worth it. Sin is never worth the price you pay, but sometimes you have to come to the end of your rope before you can see that fact.

Stuart, Melinda, and Randall had reached that point of *really* wanting help. And so they began the process of healing: admitting that what they did with their bodies was wrong and verbally declaring that they were turning away from those sins forever. That's what it means to *renounce*.

How about you? Do you want to get well? If so, what are you waiting for?

Start over today by offering your body to God as one who has been brought out of death into life (that's you!), and then offer the parts of your body to Him as instruments of righteousness.

You've got nothing to lose . . . except your bondage!

Reality Check

Ask the Lord to reveal to your mind every use of your body as an instrument of unrighteousness. Think about how you have used your eyes, ears, hands, feet, mind, mouth, and sexual organs. For each item the Lord brings to your mind, pray the following prayer out loud:

> *Lord, I confess that I have used my* (name the part of your body) *as an instrument of unrighteousness by committing the sin of* (name the sin). *I thank You for Your forgiveness and I renounce all involvement with* (name the sin). *I ask You to break any demonic bondage*

that has come into my life through that sin. In Jesus' name. Amen.

Look up the following verses in your Bible. In the blanks provided, summarize what they say about breaking the bondage of fleshly sin.

1 Peter 2:11

Romans 8:12-14

The Lie to Reject

I reject the lie that the pleasure of sin makes it worth the price of guilt, shame, and broken fellowship with my heavenly Father. I reject the lie that says "Once won't matter." I recognize that this is a trap of the devil to lure me into his cruel bondage.

The Truth to Accept

I accept the truth that freedom comes from offering my body to God as one who has been brought from death into life and that true satisfaction and lasting joy come from offering the parts of my body to God as tools for good.

Prayer for Today

Lord, I thank You that Your will indeed is good, acceptable, and perfect for me. Thank You for showing me that no matter how attractive sin may seem, it is all a cruel trap of the enemy to try to bring me into slavery to his will. I present my body to You now as a living and holy sacrifice, and I recognize that my body does not belong to me anyway. You bought me with the price of the blood of the Lord Jesus and so I belong to You. Show me today how to glorify You in my body. Amen.

Today's Bible Reading: John 8

Further Reading: 1 Corinthians 6 and 2 Timothy 2

Day 9

Too Strong to Escape

Wretched man that I am! Who will set me free from the body of this death? Thanks be to God through Jesus Christ our Lord! (Romans 7:24,25).

Harry Houdini was a master escape artist. He boasted that there were no handcuffs that could hold him, no straightjackets that could bind him, and no jail cells that could imprison him.

One day he was placed in a prison cell that had a rusty old lock. Confident that he would soon be free, Houdini retrieved a piece of metal that he had hidden on himself. This trusty tool had never failed him before, and the master was convinced that this time would be no different.

But as he set to work, he discovered that the lock was so badly corroded that it would not budge. Trying every way he knew how, Houdini labored to no avail. After several hours of failure, he fell down against the prison door, exhausted.

As his full body weight struck the door, it popped open. To his amazement, Houdini realized that the door had never been locked at all!

The apostle Paul went through a struggle for freedom in his life. He saw what God's Word said he should do, but he just couldn't bring himself to do it. He described his bondage like this in Romans 7:14,15:

> *We know that the Law is spiritual; but I am of flesh, sold into bondage to sin. For that which I am doing I do not understand; for I am not practicing what I would like to do, but I am doing the very thing I hate.*

Paul was sick of the sin that he was stuck in. Being raised as a good Jew and having come a long way already with Jesus, I'm sure Paul tried everything he could to get free. Like Houdini, he certainly had his "trusty little tool" that had always worked before. Maybe it involved praying more, fasting, memorizing Scripture, going to the synagogue, or keeping busy in the ministry.

But it all failed. In fact, Paul discovered to his horror that the more frantically he tried to stay away from things he knew were wrong, the more attractive those things became (see Romans 7:5-11).

You don't believe me? Think of the thing that you want the most but which you cannot have. Got something in mind? Okay, now try your hardest to *not* want it! You can't do it. In fact, the harder you try, the worse your obsession with the thing will become. That's what bondage is all about.

Not until we become like Houdini and give up on ourselves will we find that the door was never really locked in the first place. We just *thought* we were trapped.

Paul discovered that truth when he exhausted all his own efforts at freeing himself. Feeling about as low as it gets, he cried out for help by saying:

> *Wretched man that I am! Who will set me free from the body of this death?*

At least Paul asked the right question. It is not *"What* will set me free?" but *"Who* will set me free?"

The answer is the same for you as it was for Paul:

Thanks be to God through Jesus Christ our Lord!

Jesus is the bondage breaker. If you know Christ as Savior, He has already unlocked the door to your prison cell. Know for certain today that He alone can set you free.

Reality Check

Look up the following verses in your Bible. In the blanks provided, summarize what they say about God's desire and power to set us free.

John 8:31-36

Isaiah 61:1-3

The Lie to Reject

I reject the lie that says I am evil because I struggle with sin. I also reject the lie that says I am able to fix myself apart from the power of Christ.

The Truth to Accept

I accept the truth that Jesus Christ has set me free and

that He is the One who will enable me to walk in freedom. It is true that if Jesus sets me free, then I will be free indeed. I recognize that there is no area of bondage that is too strong for Jesus!

Prayer for Today

Lord, thank You that I am not alone in my struggles. Such a great man as the apostle Paul knew what it was like to be in bondage. Thank You for recording in Your Word his failure as well as his victory. I now recognize that no technique, strategy, or program will set me free. Only Jesus can do that. In fact, I thank You that He has already done so. Jesus won the war so that I can win my battles today over temptation and sin. In Jesus' name. Amen.

Today's Bible Reading: John 9

Further Reading: Romans 7 and Galatians 5

Day 10

On the Wings of the Spirit

Walk by the Spirit, and you will not carry out the desire of the flesh (Galatians 5:16).

I remember the first time I flew in an airplane. I was about six years old and dressed up in a new gray suit. I was flying from Newark, New Jersey, to West Palm Beach, Florida, to visit my aunt, uncle, and cousins. I was excited . . . and nervous.

I emerged from the plane several hours later with dried up Swiss steak vomit all over my brand-new suit. I'm sure I made a wonderful first impression on my relatives!

I still can't stand Swiss steak, but I have grown to like flying—especially the takeoff.

It seems like forever. First the crawling along the runway, then the waiting in line to explode into the sky—kind of like kids in a line, shuffling forward, anxiously waiting to hop on the fastest ride at an amusement park.

At last the moment comes. The pilot announces that we are "number one for takeoff." The power surges through the jet engines, roaring so loudly you almost have to shout at the person next to you to be heard.

The force of acceleration pins you back against your seat as the world races by your window. Suddenly, almost effortlessly, you lift off the ground and are airborne. Seconds later, clouds swirl around and envelop the plane and before you know it you break through into bright sunshine and brilliant blue sky.

It's incredible: Human beings normally glued to the surface of this planet by gravity are flying higher and faster than any eagle could dream. How is that possible?

It's simple: The law of aerodynamics overcomes the law of gravity. The engine thrust (power) coupled with the design of the airfoil (wings) enables the plane to overcome drag and gravity to lift up, up, and away!

The greatest thing about airline travel is that you don't have to understand any of that stuff to fly! All you have to do is climb on the plane by faith, sit in your seat, and enjoy the ride.

Believe it or not, if you are a child of God, you have a power at work in you that would make a jet engine look like an AAA battery. This power is the Holy Spirit.

Apart from God's strength, you and I would be hopelessly bound by the "gravity" of our souls—the flesh. The flesh is like the toxic waste left over from our B.C. (before Christ) days. It produces stuff in us such as jealousy, anger, envy, quarreling, drunkenness, sexual sin, rebellion, lying, cheating, and other gunk (see Galatians 5:19-21).

But the power of the Holy Spirit is stronger than the power of the flesh. And if we, by faith, choose to rely on that higher power, we will soar in our Christian lives like a jet airplane.

The results of relying on God's mighty power instead of our own flesh will be good stuff such as "love, joy, peace, patience, kindness, goodness, faithfulness, gentleness, and self control" (Galatians 5:22,23).

The choice is yours. You can be like a crazy person and

decide to take a walk outside the airplane! If you do, you'll find that the law of gravity is still in effect. The flesh will rear its ugly head real fast if you stop trusting in the Spirit's power to live the Christian life.

Or you can stop fighting a losing battle and climb aboard, sit down, and enjoy the ride. The power of the Holy Spirit will enable you to soar with Jesus.

So why not sit down today and buckle up? We're "number one" for takeoff!

Reality Check

Do you think your life usually shows evidence of the flesh or of the Spirit being in control? (Look up Galatians 5:19-23 if you're not sure.)

It's incredible to think that God Himself lives inside you through the Holy Spirit, but He does! Since God is all-powerful, what are some of the changes He is willing and able to make in your life?

Pick one area under the "fruit of the Spirit" (Galatians 5:22,23) that you really need to work on. Take some time to pray, asking God to produce that aspect of His character in you.

Look up the following verses in your Bible. In the blanks provided, summarize what they say about living according to the Spirit and not according to the flesh.

Galatians 5:24-26

Romans 8:12-17

The Lie to Reject

I reject the lie that says the Christian life works for others but it doesn't work for me. I reject the lie of Satan that tells me I am doomed to be a slave of my flesh the rest of my life and that I will never change.

The Truth to Accept

I accept the truth that through the power of the Holy Spirit I can say no to the desires of my flesh and walk in the newness of life in Christ. I agree that real change is possible in my life as I continue to choose to live by the Spirit's power.

PRAYER FOR TODAY

Lord, I thank You for coming to live inside me through the presence and power of the Holy Spirit. I indeed am your temple. I choose today to give up indulging the desires of my flesh, and I choose instead to walk by faith hand in hand with Your Spirit. I thank You that He will give me the power to live life in a way that pleases You. I look forward to the fruit of the Spirit ripening and sweetening in my life as I live by Your power. In Jesus' name. Amen.

TODAY'S BIBLE READING: John 10

FURTHER READING: John 16 and Acts 2

Day 11

Hang Tough . . . Jesus Did!

Discipline yourself for the purpose of godliness; for bodily discipline is only of little profit, but godliness is profitable for all things, since it holds promise for the present life and also for the life to come (1 Timothy 4:7,8).

She was at the top of her game and number one in the world. But at age 19 she was as unpredictable as the weather. What color would her hair be? What would she wear? Would she even show up to play?

As a teenager her behavior was erratic, but as a tennis player her two-handed backhands and forehands were consistently explosive. Punctuated by those famous groans and giggles, she breathed more life into women's tennis than anyone since Chris Evert.

But in April of 1993 life came crashing down around Monica Seles. A stab wound in her back at the hand of a German lathe operator named Guenther Parche ended it all . . . or so it appeared.

The stab wound took six months to heal, but the emotions have taken much longer. In spite of it all, however, Monica is back.[1]

As of this writing, she has already trounced Gabriela Sabatini and Amanda Coetzer to win the Canadian Open. And barring any further injuries, this is likely just the beginning of Monica's "second" career in pro tennis.

How could she have made such a comeback? Obviously, Monica Seles has incredible talent. There is no doubt about that. But beyond her giftedness there has been hard work. Who knows how many thousands of hours of mental suffering, emotional agony, and painful physical therapy and training she has endured over the last two or three years? But the tennis world is thrilled she's made it.

What do you discipline yourself for? God says training your body is "only of little profit." That's a pretty remarkable statement considering how much money many athletes make!

But in contrast to disciplining yourself "for the purpose of godliness," all the running, weight training, aerobics, sports practices, watching of diet, and so on, pale in comparison.

Why? Because when you discipline your body, it benefits you for only a short time here on earth. But when you discipline yourself to become like Christ, it pays dividends for here and for eternity!

We've really missed it big time in our sports-crazy country, and I'm sure it's the same story at your school. Who gets the applause and the honor and the rewards? The star athletes, of course. But what about the guy who faithfully attends a Bible club or the girl who prays with others around the flagpole in September or the teenage couple who commit themselves to staying sexually pure until marriage?

No awards at banquets for them. No newspaper articles. No announcements over the school P.A. system. No scholarships. No expectations of big bucks from professional contracts. No product commercials.

But long after the applause of this world dies down and others take the athlete's place of honor, and long after the athlete's rewards rust and decay, the child of God who hangs in there with Jesus will still stand.

You see, the real banquet in heaven hasn't begun yet. The eternal awards haven't been given out yet. The Lord Jesus Christ hasn't yet announced those priceless words, "Well done, good and faithful slave; you were faithful with a few things, I will put you in charge of many things; enter into the joy of your master" (Matthew 25:23).

Will it be hard? Yes, at times. It had to be terribly hard for Monica Seles to keep from chucking it all when the pain in her back screamed every time she moved and the fear of what might happen again gnawed at her soul.

Spiritual discipline is never easy. But God's Word says it is well worth it. Maybe you are clawing your way back to God after a serious injury to your soul. Maybe you are tired of being different and going against the flow of immorality around you. Don't give up. Fix your eyes on the One who endured the agony of hanging on the cross for you. He knows what you're going through.

So hang tough . . . Jesus did!

Reality Check

What parts of the Christian life do you find hard to practice regularly? Is it reading the Bible, praying, attending church, attending youth group activities, memorizing Scripture, forgiving others, or sharing your faith? Why do you feel it's hard to stay disciplined in these areas?

What benefits can you see coming to your life if you are consistent in the areas mentioned previously? What possible consequences could come to your life if you become lazy in these areas?

Remember, God loves you whether you discipline yourself spiritually or not. He has provided these things, however, to help you grow in faith, hope, and love. How important is it to you to grow strong spiritually and become more and more like Jesus?

Look up the following verses in your Bible. In the blanks provided, summarize what they say about the benefits of spiritual discipline.

Psalm 1:1-3

Philippians 4:6-9

The Lie to Reject

I reject the lie that says I will be happiest taking the easy, comfortable road in life. I recognize that the devil does not want me to discipline myself spiritually, and that he wants me to think it is not worth the effort. I reject the lie that I am too undisciplined to live the Christian life.

The Truth to Accept

I accept the truth that disciplining myself spiritually is more important than disciplining myself physically, because its rewards go beyond this life into eternity. I accept the truth that, through the power of the Holy Spirit, I can be self-controlled (Galatians 5:23) *and that God has not given me a spirit of fear, but of power, love and discipline* (2 Timothy 1:7).

Prayer for Today

Lord, I have been willing in the past to work hard at achieving goals in life—whether in sports, school, relationships, money, jobs, music, drama, or art. Forgive me for being lazy in my relationship with You, thinking it was not really worth making the effort. I recognize now that I had bought into the world's value system. Help me to know how to give proper emphasis to these other activities and pursuits while making You the number one priority in my time and energy. In Jesus' name. Amen.

Today's Bible Reading: John 11

Further Reading: 1 Corinthians 9 and Hebrews 12

Day 12

Not Even a Close Second

Jesus came to them and said, "All authority in heaven and on earth has been given to me" (Matthew 28:18 NIV).

I had always wanted to be a secret agent, and one hot, sweaty day in August I had my chance.

I had just left the Brother Andrew office in Hong Kong and was headed for the border of Red China. Loaded up with a healthy supply of New Testaments, hymnals, and gospel tracts placed inside several pieces of luggage, I tried not to look suspicious. But as I walked toward the train station I couldn't help but wonder if I were being watched. The butterflies in my stomach danced and fluttered as I imagined angry border guards slashing open my bags and interrogating me under bright lights.

Actually I was in little physical danger, though the possibility of those precious pieces of life-giving truth being confiscated at the border was very real. I thought of the desperate need to get the gospel into that country of one billion people, and I began to pray.

"Lord, get this material through to the people who need it," I asked God silently as the train rumbled on through the lush, green mountains.

I remembered the famous prayer that Brother Andrew had uttered so many years before: "Lord, while You walked this earth You made blind eyes see. Now make seeing eyes blind."

I knew that only about two-thirds of the bags made it past the searching eyes of the border guards, and so I prayed more earnestly.

After purchasing my visa to enter Communist China, I stood in line to cross the border. Adrenaline started to flow. I could feel the tension in the air.

All carry-ons had to be placed on the conveyor belt which would pass under the scrutiny of the X-ray machine. "Will the clothes I stuffed around the literature disguise what is really inside my bags?" I wondered as I plopped the pieces on the belt.

The moment of truth had come. I strode confidently forward, not wanting to cause any suspicion.

All of a sudden the two border guards who were inspecting the X-ray monitor started cracking up! One of them must have told the joke of the century. Their cigarette-clutching hands pounded their knees as their heads flew back in laughter... just as my bags passed under the X-ray machine!

The two men had seen nothing. My bags filled with treasure emerged on the other side of the belt, safe and sound. No angry guards with guns running toward me. No sirens sounding. Nothing.

I was so excited I wanted to pump my fists into the air and shout "Hallelujah!" from the top of my lungs. Realizing that this would not be a very good idea, I calmly exited the train station instead. Within an hour the drop-off had been made without incident. I never saw the Chinese Christian who picked up the material (much too dangerous for him), but my mission was accomplished. God had opened a door that no man could shut.

The bad news is that there are many enemies of the cross of Christ, both human and spiritual. The good news is that Jesus is on the throne and no plan of His can be thwarted. He is in control.

Jesus Himself put it this way: "*All* authority has been given to me in heaven and on earth." In other words, Jesus calls the shots and there is no one who can say to Him, "Uh-uh. Ain't gonna happen."

Try a little first-grade math with me for a moment. If Jesus has all authority in heaven, how much authority in heaven does the devil have? Well, none, of course!

And if Jesus has all authority on earth, how much authority on earth does the devil have? Right again . . . zip, zilch, nada.

Even when things don't go as we would like them to, God is in control. There is not one microsecond when He is not in control. You can be confident that in the end God will win out. He always does.

Isn't it time we stop bowing in fear to the devil and start bowing in worship to the King? Jesus the King of kings and Lord of lords has all authority in heaven and on earth. The devil? He's not even a close second.

Reality Check

What does it mean to you that Jesus has all authority in heaven and on earth?

When tough times hit, how will knowing that God is in control help you stick it out?

Is there any way in which you have allowed the fear of people or Satan to keep you from doing what's right? Confess that behavior to the Lord right now and ask Him to open your eyes to how powerful and sovereign He really is.

Look up the following verse in your Bible (it's dynamite!) and jot down all the words or phrases that show how powerful Jesus is.

Ephesians 1:18-23

The Lie to Reject

I reject the lie that says the devil has any right or authority to control my life. I reject any thought or feeling of helplessness, hopelessness, or abandonment by God as a lie from the pit of hell.

The Truth to Accept

I accept the truth that all (not a little, some, or most), but all authority in heaven and on earth belongs to Jesus. I choose to walk by faith in that truth, even when it seems like the devil is winning. I affirm that in the end Jesus will win out, because He is the King, and He is in ultimate control.

Prayer for Today

Father, I thank You that the Lord Jesus sits at Your right hand, far above all rule and authority and power and dominion, and every name that ever was, is, or will be. I thank You that all things are under the feet of Jesus, and that Jesus has already won the war over Satan. Please strengthen me to keep my eyes on these truths today no matter how rough the battle becomes. I know You will enable me to endure hardship because Jesus endured the cross for me. In His name I pray. Amen.

TODAY'S BIBLE READING: John 12

FURTHER READING: Colossians 2 and 1 John 3

Day 13

Welcome to the Winning Side

God raised us up with Christ and seated us with him in the heavenly realms in Christ Jesus (Ephesians 2:6 NIV).

During World War Two, Lieutenant General Jonathan Mayhew Wainwright was commander of the Allied Forces in the Philippines. Following a heroic resistance of enemy forces, he was forced to surrender the island of Corregidor to the Japanese on May 6, 1942. He, along with many others, was taken captive by the enemy.

For three years he suffered terribly as a prisoner of war in a camp in Manchuria, China. During that time he endured a constant barrage of almost unbelievable cruelty—malnutrition, physical and emotional abuse, and relentless psychological mind-games.

Throughout the three years of imprisonment, Wainwright somehow maintained his dignity as a human being and soldier. But incredibly, even after the Japanese surrendered to end World War Two, his captors kept him and other American prisoners behind bars! The war was over, but their bondage continued.

One day an Allied plane landed in a field near the prison, and through the fence that surrounded the prison an airman informed the general of the news: Japan had surrendered and victory was ours!

Wainwright immediately pulled his frail and weakened body to attention, then turned and marched toward the Japanese command house. He burst through the door and marched up to the camp's commanding officer.

"My Commander-in-Chief has conquered your Commander-in-Chief. I am now in charge of this camp," Wainwright declared.

In response, the Japanese officer took off his sword, laid it on the table, and surrendered his command.

What a powerful picture of the authority we have in Christ! Our Commander-in-Chief, the Lord Jesus Christ, came to destroy the works of the devil (1 John 3:8), and He succeeded! The war has been won, and we share in Christ's victory.

You see, the right hand of God is the seat of authority in heaven. That's where Jesus is (Ephesians 1:20; Hebrews 1:3). We have been raised up and seated with Christ (Ephesians 2:6). Therefore we share the authority that Christ has over the evil one!

At first, Lieutenant General Wainwright didn't realize that the Allies had won the war, and so he remained in prison. But when he found out that he was on the winning side he marched by faith over to the Japanese commander's office and took over. The conquered officer had no choice but to surrender.

Wainwright probably did not *feel* all that victorious when he stormed into that office. Three years of horrible conditions had probably drained most of the life out of him. But he acted boldly on what he knew to be true: The Japanese had been defeated.

Maybe you have lived under a cloud of defeat and despair behind the bars of a jail made of Satan's lies.

Don't you think it's about time you stormed into the devil's strongholds in your life? Don't you think it's about time you tell him you're sick and tired of being controlled by a defeated foe? Don't you think it's about time you announce to him that Jesus won the war and that he must surrender his command?

The Lord Jesus Christ is the conquering Commander-in-Chief. And you? You are His general. Satan is a defeated foe.

Let those truths set you free today. And welcome to the winning side!

Reality Check

Look up the following verses in your Bible. In the blanks provided, summarize what they say about Christ's victory over Satan and what effect this should have on our lives.

Colossians 2:13-15 (Note: "rulers and authorities" refers to demonic forces).

Hebrews 2:14,15

The Lie to Reject

I reject the lie that my being "raised up and seated with Christ" is simply a future position with no effect on my life today. I refuse to believe the enemy's attempts to get me to believe that I do not have authority over him in Christ.

The Truth to Accept

I accept the truth that I am in Christ right now. I affirm that I have not only been crucified with Him and raised to walk in newness of life with Him but that I also have been seated with Him at the Father's right hand. Because of my position in Christ right now, I announce that the Lord Jesus Christ shares with me His victory and authority over the enemy.

Prayer for Today

Dear heavenly Father, what a privilege it is to be called Your child, and that is what I want to focus on in my life. I don't want to be demon-centered. I want to be Christ-centered.

I thank You that in Christ I have authority over the enemy, but I choose to rejoice that my name is written in heaven (Luke 10:20). *Please teach me how to exercise the authority that Christ has given me so that I can help build Your kingdom by making disciples and setting captives free.*

In Jesus' powerful name I pray. Amen.

TODAY'S BIBLE READING: John 13

FURTHER READING: Mark 9 and Luke 10

Day 14

Jesus Ain't No Magic Wand!

God is opposed to the proud, but gives grace to the humble. Submit therefore to God. Resist the devil and he will flee from you (James 4:6,7).

Sometimes truth is stranger than fiction. The following story, as wild as it is, does not come from a Frank Peretti novel. It comes right out of the Bible. It's the kind of stuff great movies are made of. Let's tune in on the action as Dr. Luke recorded it in Acts 19:13-20 NIV because there is a crucial lesson for us to learn right here in twentieth-century America.

> *Some Jews who went around driving out evil spirits tried to invoke the name of the Lord Jesus over those who were demon-possessed. They would say, "In the name of Jesus, whom Paul preaches, I command you to come out." Seven sons of Sceva, a Jewish chief priest, were doing this. One day, the evil spirit answered them, "Jesus I know, and I know about Paul, but who are you?" Then the man who had the evil spirit jumped on them and overpowered them all. He*

> *gave them such a beating that they ran out of the house naked and bleeding. When this became known to the Jews and Greeks living in Ephesus, they were all seized with fear, and the name of the Lord Jesus was held in high honor. Many of those who believed now came and openly confessed their evil deeds. A number who had practiced sorcery brought their scrolls together and burned them publicly. When they calculated the value of the scrolls, the total came to fifty thousand drachmas [millions and millions of dollars]. In this way the word of the Lord spread widely and grew in power.*

What an incredible display of God's power! Here was a totally disastrous attempt at helping a demonized person, and the Lord turned it into a revival!

There are a couple of points in this passage of Scripture that we dare not miss.

First, look what happened to those who acted like Christians but were not. The seven sons of Sceva had no relationship with God and were not followers of Christ. And they got thoroughly thrashed. Even when the seven dropped the name of Paul in there for good measure, it didn't help. In essence the demon said, "Oh, we know Jesus all right, and Paul has been a pain in the neck to us, but who are you guys?" The result was not a pretty sight.

Second, look what happened *to those who believed*. They openly confessed their sin and publicly burned their sorcery scrolls. Why? Because they knew they had been hiding their sin and were set up to get thrashed as well. They realized that only by "cleaning house" spiritually could they be protected by the power of the name of Jesus.

James put it this way: "Submit therefore to God. Resist the devil and he will flee from you." The order of those commands is critical. First you submit to God, and then you resist the devil. You can try to resist the devil until you are blue in the face, but if you have not first surrendered your life to Christ's lordship, the devil won't budge.

How about it? Are you living under the authority of God in your life? Be warned! You cannot exercise spiritual authority *for* God until you are under spiritual authority *from* God.

Maybe you're saying, "Well, I'm a Christian; isn't that enough?" No! If you are living in pride, rebellion, bitterness, or bondage to sins of the flesh, you might as well paint a bull's-eye on your chest and say to the devil, "Here I am!"

Why not be wise like those in Ephesus who came clean before God? Confess your sins and get rid of anything that ties you to your past life of sin.

And remember the painful lesson of the seven sons of Sceva: The name of Jesus is not a magic wand you can wave. To *exercise* authority, you must be *under* authority.

Reality Check

What does it mean to "submit" to God?

Why is it so important to first submit to God before you try to resist the devil?

Ask the Lord to reveal to your mind any areas of your life in which you are proudly refusing to let Jesus control. Confess those areas of sin to God and get rid of anything that ties you to them. Do it today. Better yet, do it *now.*

The Lie to Reject

I reject the lie that says that just because I am a Christian, I have a magic bubble of protection around me against the devil. I reject the lie that I can do whatever I want and God will somehow protect me from all pain and consequences.

The Truth to Accept

I accept the truth that living my life in total submission to the lordship of Christ is the only path to spiritual protection. I recognize that as I live under the authority of God I can then exercise that authority by resisting the devil and he will flee from me.

Prayer for Today

Dear Lord, I understand that there are certain things You expect me to do to live a victorious Christian life. One of them is to put every area of my life under Your direction. I choose to do that right now—to present my body as a living and holy sacrifice to You. I want to live under Your authority. As I continue to do so, show me how to resist the attacks of the enemy in my life. May the name of Jesus be held in high honor and may the word of the Lord spread widely and grow in power because of my life. I humble myself before You, Lord, and trust in Your all-sufficient grace. Amen.

Today's Bible Reading: John 14

Further Reading: Luke 7 and Acts 4

Day 15

This Means War!

> *Though we live in the world, we do not wage war as the world does. The weapons we fight with are not the weapons of the world. On the contrary, they have divine power to demolish strongholds* (2 Corinthians 10:3,4 NIV).

A pizza place is a weird site for a war to break out, but that is exactly what happened.

I was sharing the gospel with Jonathan, a high school student with whom I had been building a friendship. He was a nice kid who played in the school band. Unfortunately, he had gotten himself mixed up in the drug scene and was also having sex with his girlfriend.

When I had met with Jonathan the previous week, he expressed concern that if he gave his life to Christ his friends would reject him. I asked him now if that issue was still bothering him.

"Nah, that doesn't bother me anymore. I really don't care what they say. I need to do what I think is right."

I was encouraged by his sincere response, so I probed some more. "Well, Jonathan, can you think of any reason why you couldn't receive Jesus Christ as your Savior and Lord?"

His face looked puzzled and there was a bit of frustration in his voice as he said, "I don't know. Something just keeps telling me to put it off for awhile."

Immediately I knew what (or rather who!) that "something" was. War was starting to break out in Jonathan's mind, and I needed to attack with the spiritual weapons I had.

"Jonathan, I know it might seem a little strange in a pizza place, but could I pray for you right now?" I had already looked around, and we were pretty much alone.

"I guess," he replied, shrugging his shoulders.

"Father, in the name of Jesus, I pray that Satan would be bound right now in Jonathan's life so that he can open his heart to Christ," I began, standing on the authority I had in the Lord Jesus.

As I continued praying for Jonathan, I felt an attack of fierce hatred and anger pouring across the table toward me. I opened my eyes for a brief instant and was relieved to see Jonathan's head bowed and eyes closed.

By the time I had finished praying, that sense of attack had lifted and a tremendous joy and peace flooded my heart.

"Are you ready to receive Jesus now?" I asked him, smiling.

"Yes, I am," Jonathan responded excitedly. He added, "When you were praying for me, I felt like I was going to cry all over this table!"

Jonathan became a child of God that day.

What was going on in his head? An intense spiritual battle for his mind was taking place. No amount of arguing, persuading, pushing, or encouraging on my part would have made a lick of difference. Why not? Because a spiritual war requires spiritual weapons!

What was needed was God's power, not my power, to set Jonathan free to receive Jesus as Savior. And the prayer of faith prayed in the authority of the name of Jesus is the nuclear warhead of spiritual battle! And in this case that "bomb" hit the target!

Don't ever think, however, that spiritual battle happens only with non-Christians. Jonathan, sincere in his newfound faith in Christ, had major struggles with drugs and sexual immorality to overcome. The battle had just begun!

What does it mean when you become a Christian? It means new life, forgiveness, eternal life, new power, faith, hope, and love. But it also means war.

REALITY CHECK

When you hear the term "spiritual battle," what comes to your mind?

What do you think are the weapons God has given us to wage spiritual battle? What makes them so powerful?

Are you struggling with a battle for your mind today? Find a trusted friend to pray with you as you walk through the Steps to Freedom in Christ. (If you aren't familiar with these steps, see *The Bondage Breaker Youth Edition.*)

Look up the following verses in your Bible. In the blanks provided, summarize what they say about spiritual battle.

Romans 8:35-37

Romans 13:11-14

The Lie to Reject

I reject the lie that says the mental and emotional battles I experience are purely psychological. I cannot defeat the enemy's spiritual attacks by fleshly weapons that the world uses.

The Truth to Accept

I accept the truth that as a believer in Christ I am subject to spiritual attacks that affect my mind and emotions. I also accept the truth that the spiritual weapons God has given me are loaded with God's power to destroy the devil's strongholds (fortresses of deception) in my life.

Prayer for Today

Dear heavenly Father, thank You for saving me and adopting me into Your family. I thank You that my place in Your heart and home is secure. I look forward to the day when I can come home and be safe in Your arms forever. Until that day, however, I thank You that You have given me the privilege to serve as a soldier behind enemy lines. I consider it an honor to wage war for King Jesus. Thank You, too, for the incredibly powerful spiritual weapons You have given me. Teach me each day, Lord, how to use them effectively for Your glory. In Jesus' victorious name, I pray. Amen.

TODAY'S BIBLE READING: John 15

FURTHER READING: 2 Kings 6 and 2 Chronicles 20

Day 16

Prisoners of War

We are destroying speculations and every lofty thing raised up against the knowledge of God, and we are taking every thought captive to the obedience of Christ (2 Corinthians 10:5).

A student named Jay had an experience that shows how deceptive Satan's thoughts can be. Jay came into my office one day and said, "Dr. Anderson, I'm in trouble."

"What's the problem, Jay?"

"When I sit down to study I get prickly sensations all over my body, my vision gets blurry, and I can't concentrate."

"Tell me about your walk with God," I probed.

"I have a very close walk with God," Jay boasted.

"What do you mean?"

"Well, when I leave school at noon each day, I ask God where He wants me to go for lunch. If I hear a thought that says 'Burger King,' I go to Burger King. Then I ask Him what He wants me to eat. If the thought comes to order a Whopper, I order a Whopper."

"What about your church attendance?" I continued.

"I go every Sunday wherever God tells me to go. And for the last three Sundays God has told me to go to a Mormon church."

I immediately knew Satan was invading Jay's thoughts because God would never direct a Christian to a church with a twisted doctrine of Christ and God's Word.

Jay sincerely wanted to do God's will but he was listening to his thoughts as if they were God's voice instead of "taking every thought captive to the obedience of Christ." He had opened himself up to Satan's schemes in his life.[1]

Think of your mind as the command post of your life. In military life, the command post is the nerve center, the strategic hub where decisions are made. Security around such a place is airtight.

Should you not have the same kind of tight security around your mind? Of course you should. But to do so you must take active control of the thoughts that pass in and out of your brain.

Recognize that the thoughts, ideas, and attitudes you have may be friend or foe. Some ideas and beliefs that you hold are from God and therefore are true. Others are not.

Hang on to the ones that are true. Disregard the ones that are false and, through God's Word, replace them with truth.

Remember, you are in a war, and the battle is for your mind. Like an alert border patrol, learn to take captive every thought as it first enters your mind. Treat it as a prisoner of war until you determine whether it is the truth or a lie. A more mature Christian can help you with the thoughts that are tough to figure out.

Beware especially of *speculations*. They can be very dangerous. A speculation would be trying to figure out a person's motives for acting a certain way. You will usually be wrong. Another speculation would be trying to figure out how God will or should work out a tough problem. He's usually got a better way!

Beware also of *lofty things raised up against the knowledge of God.* Any opinion, philosophy, or idea that goes against the character of God or the truth of His Word is evil, no matter how good it may sound.

So, learn to say, "Stop—who goes there?" to the thoughts that seek to enter your mind. Embrace the good ones as friends, and send the ones that are foes on their way... right away!

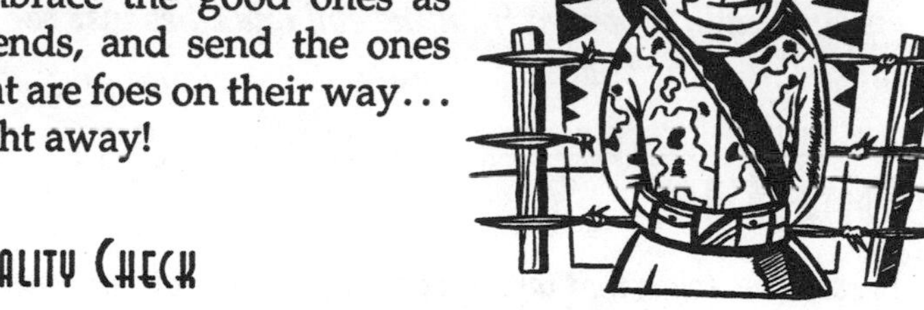

Reality Check

Why is it important to keep watch over the thoughts that come into your mind?

What are some ways you can tell if a new thought, idea, or attitude that you have is true and right or not?

Look up the following verses in your Bible. In the blanks provided, summarize what they say about keeping close tabs on your thought life.

Romans 12:1-3

1 Peter 1:13

The Lie to Reject

I reject the lie that says I can be passive and lazy with my thought life and just "go with the flow," and still be spiritually strong. I reject the lie that says my mind is automatically protected from the evil one's lies just because I'm a Christian.

The Truth to Accept

I accept the truth that taking every thought captive to the obedience of Christ is essential for my spiritual health and freedom. I recognize that not everything that comes to my mind is true, and so I accept the responsibility to monitor my thought life under the direction and power of God.

Prayer for Today

Dear Father, I thank You for giving me my mind. I also thank You that through the enabling power of the Holy Spirit I can have the strength and endurance to keep tabs on my thought life. I choose today to gird my mind for action and stay sober in spirit. I ask for discernment to recognize the lies that come into my mind from my flesh and the devil. Please empower me to be a faithful student of Your Word so that I can quickly distinguish truth from error. In Jesus' name. Amen.

TODAY'S BIBLE READING: John 16

FURTHER READING: James 1 and James 3

Day 17

Let's Bury Worry

Humble yourselves, therefore, under the mighty hand of God, that He may exalt you at the proper time, casting all your anxiety upon Him, because He cares for you (1 Peter 5:6,7).

Worry. It ruled the life of California artist J.H. Zorthian. After reading a news story about a small boy who was hit and killed by a car, he vowed that he would never allow such a tragedy to happen to any of his three kids.

Day by day his anxiety grew. The more he thought about losing one of his children, the more his worry possessed him—dominating his thoughts and sapping away his life as an artist.

Finally he ditched his plans to build a big house in crowded Pasadena and opted instead for a remote mountain home. He bought 12 acres at the end of a long, winding road, far from civilization. And at every turn in the road he posted a "Children at Play" sign.

Even before he started on the house, he constructed a fenced-in yard for his kids. The play area was completely safe and secure from any cars.

Then came the house. It was a work of art and a haven

of safety. But it became a monument to Zorthian's obsession with protecting his kids from any and all harm; it was an altar to the gods of insecurity, worry, and control that had come to run his life.

He had a one-car garage built so that no one but he personally would ever drive in and out of it. But there was only one problem: He had to back out of the garage. That posed the possibility of not being able to see one of his kids and accidentally backing over him. That hazard would have to be removed.

The solution? Build a turnaround in the driveway. The plans were made to pour the concrete for the project, but the first rainfall in weeks halted the work.

If everything had gone according to plan, the turnaround would have been finished and usable by Sunday, February 9. But that day, the ninth day of February, would forever be burned into the memory of J.H. Zorthian. For that was the day his one-and-a-half-year-old son, Tiran, wriggled out from his sister's arms and ran behind the car as Zorthian backed out of his garage.

Every anxious effort to control circumstances and provide a totally safe, secure environment for his children died that day under the wheels of Mr. Zorthian's car.

J.H. Zorthian had the best of intentions: He wanted his children to be safe. But he went about it the wrong way. He thought he could control life and forgot that the buck stops with God, not man.

That's why Peter encouraged us to humble ourselves under God's mighty hand. We need to stop trying to control people and circumstances. We're playing God when we do that, and we won't do a very good job. I know. I've tried.

Peter also exhorted us to drop all our worries in God's lap. He can handle them. Stop worrying about money, your family, your future, your relationships, your grades, and anything else you're uptight about. Why? Because God cares for you.

So what are you worried about today? Why not pray and give those things to God right now? Thank Him that He can more than handle the toughest things you face.

While you're young and free (I hope!) from migraines, ulcers, high blood pressure, burnout, and other stress-related maladies, learn to trust God with your troubles, and live a responsible life before Him.

Bury your worries before they bury you.

Reality Check

Think about the things you have been worried about. In what ways have you been trying to control people or circumstances rather than trusting in God?

What is the connection between *humbling yourself before God* and *being free from worry and anxiety?*

Since worry demonstrates a lack of trust in God, it is a sin. Ask the Lord right now to reveal to your mind all the ways you have given in to anxious thoughts. As He brings those things to mind, confess them to God in prayer.

Look up the following verses in your Bible. In the blanks

provided, summarize what they say about trusting God versus being worried.

Philippians 4:6,7

Matthew 6:33,34

The Lie to Reject

I reject the lie that says it's okay to live my life filled with worry and anxiety. I refuse to let my insecurities control me just because that's the way most people live. It is still wrong.

The Truth to Accept

I accept the truth that I can cast my anxieties on the Lord because He cares for me. I affirm that as I pray about my concerns with thanksgiving, God will replace my worry with peace that will guard my heart and mind in Christ Jesus.

Prayer for Today

Lord, thank You that You are faithful. Thank You that

You are big and strong and that You can handle everything that comes my way. Please forgive me for the times I have felt driven to control people or circumstances around me. I confess that the habit of "playing God" and the root cause of that sin is my pride. I humble myself before You, releasing all my life into Your hands. Thank You that You have promised to exalt me at the proper time and to care for me all the time. I thank You for Your peace which calms my heart and stills my soul. In Jesus' name. Amen.

TODAY'S BIBLE READING: John 17

FURTHER READING: Matthew 6 and Philippians 4

Day 18

The Lyin' Lion

Be of sober spirit, be on the alert. Your adversary, the devil, prowls about like a roaring lion, seeking someone to devour (1 Peter 5:8).

I hope you never have the misfortune of seeing a demon. It's not a pleasant experience, believe me. It happened to me one quiet July night at a beach resort.

I was on a summer mission project with a bunch of high school students and youth leaders. To be honest with you, things were not going very well. A number of the kids were rebelling big-time against God and the leadership. Anger, bitterness, apathy, and even some stealing were the order of the day.

The devil was having a field day.

That night I was minding my own business, lying on my back, happily asleep in bed, when I was awakened. And there, perched in midair right above my head, was this ugly, laughing, mocking face. And it wasn't one of the teenagers either!

I'm a red-blooded American man and a child of God who has been raised up with Christ to the right hand of the Father. So what did I do?

I freaked out, pulled the sheet up over my head, prayed, and tried to get back to sleep, hoping it would go away![1]

I found out years later that I am not alone in this experience. Many people I've met and counseled complain of "panic attacks"—often at night, but sometimes in the daytime as well. These are times when they are gripped by a suffocating terror that seems to come from nowhere and everywhere.

Our ministry did a survey a few years ago of 1725 Christian junior and senior high students. Nearly half of them said they had seen or heard a presence in their room that scared them![2]

What is going on? These attacks are intimidation tactics from the biggest bully of them all—the devil. Satan and his demons use fear as one of their main weapons against Christians.

The devil knows that if he can scare the living daylights out of you, then you are much less likely to stand up to him. And he also knows (maybe even better than you do!) that in Christ you have authority over him. He cannot rob you of that authority, but if he can paralyze you with fear so that you do not use your authority, he has accomplished the same thing!

Satan is pictured in Scripture as a roaring lion, prowling around, looking for someone to devour. The roar of a lion is a terrifying sound that can freeze its prey with fear. Then the stalking predator can pounce upon its victim and devour it.

Unfortunately, the devil is eating too many frightened believers in Christ for lunch! Just as the lion tries to isolate the weak and sickly from the herd, since they're much easier to catch, so the devil attacks the spiritually weak.

How do you deal with a bully who is bugging you?

You bring somebody along with you who can beat the snot out of him! Then you'll watch the bully become what he really is . . . a coward!

Don't try to stand against the devil by yourself. When fear strikes, call on the Lord Jesus to strengthen you. Then tell the enemy to beat it in the name of Jesus, and watch him run!

That's what I should have done that quiet summer night at the beach. At that time I was scared of the devil, but now I know better. I have since learned that nowhere in the Bible are we told to fear Satan. He is a defeated foe who tries to frighten us into trembling before him. Don't be deceived. He's just a lyin' lion!

Reality Check

Look up the following verses in your Bible. In the blanks provided, summarize what they say about overcoming fear or timidity.

2 Timothy 1:7

Isaiah 41:10

The Lie to Reject

I reject all fear and intimidation tactics from the devil, because God has not given me a spirit of fear, but of power, love, and a sound mind.

The Truth to Accept

I accept the truth that Satan has been defeated by the Lord Jesus and that in Christ I have authority over the devil. I choose to stay spiritually alert and to resist all efforts of the enemy to intimidate me through fear.

Prayer for Today

Lord, I recognize the very real danger of being swallowed up by the devil's attacks of fear and anxiety. I thank You, Lord, for the encouragement from Your Word that reminds me I don't need to fear because You are with me. I don't need to give in to anxiety because You are my God. You have promised to strengthen me, help me, and uphold me with Your righteous right hand. Thank You for the power, love, and sound mind that You have given me to resist the devil's roaring attacks of fear. I pray in faith in the unbeatable name of Jesus. Amen.

Today's Bible Reading: John 18

Further Reading: Psalm 27 and 1 Peter 5

Day 19

No Sting Operation

O Death, where is your victory? O Death, where is your sting? The sting of death is sin, and the power of sin is the law; but thanks be to God, who gives us the victory through our Lord Jesus Christ (1 Corinthians 15:55-57).

It was a beautiful day in early June. The whole world was alive with color. Every tree shouted to the world that new life had come, broadcasting in every brilliant shade of green imaginable. The sky was a windswept blue, punctuated with white puffball cumulus clouds. And the roses filled in the gaps of every rainbow color that the trees and sky missed.

Dad and his little girl, Rebecca, decided to take a ride in the country to soak up the late spring morning. He rolled down the window, breathed in a great gulp of fresh, cool air, and took off down the deserted back road.

A few miles into their journey, Dad noticed Rebecca getting upset. "What's wrong, Honey?" he asked her gently.

"There's a bee in here, Daddy. Do something!"

Rebecca was horribly allergic to bee stings and had to take medication with her wherever she went. But even with the treatment on hand, being stung was a terrifying experience for the little girl—one to be avoided if at all possible.

As Dad brought the car to a skidding halt, he looked over at Rebecca and saw that fear had taken over. She was frantically slapping at the air as the honeybee buzzed around her head.

And then it was over just as quickly as it had begun.

"Daddy, what happened to the bee? I don't hear buzzing anymore?" Rebecca's eyes were darting around, certain to see the bee sitting somewhere, ready to attack. But the bee was gone.

"I took care of it, Sweetheart. See?"

To Rebecca's horror, her dad opened his clenched fist and the bee flew out, taking one quick buzz around the car before exiting through the open window.

"Dad, why did you let that awful thing out in the car again? It could've stung me!"

"No, Rebecca. Once it left my hand, it was harmless to you. You see, when I grabbed it, it stung *me*. See? You can still see the stinger in the palm of my hand. That's how honeybees are made. They can sting only once, and then they fly away to die."

When we read in the newspaper that a group of partying teens is killed in a fiery car crash, it makes us stop and think. When we hear that one of our classmates takes her own life, we wonder where she is now. As we watch a loved one waste away from cancer, it can (and should!) cause us to realize that there are no guarantees for any of us.

When we're young we think we're immortal and invincible. We protect ourselves from the reality of death by convincing ourselves, "That won't happen to me," and then we get busy so we don't have to think about it anymore.

But the Bible tells us that "it is appointed for men to die once, and after this comes judgment" (Hebrews 9:27).

When is your appointment? When is mine? It could be today. It could be (at least for you!) 70 or 80 years from now. We simply do not know.

But does this mean we have to fear death? No! Absolutely not! Jesus took the sting out of death for us. Because He died, we who trust in Him to save us have the assurance that heaven is our final destination.

Yes, unless Jesus comes back first, you and I will die one day. But thanks be to God, who gives us the victory over death through our Lord Jesus Christ! You don't believe me? Just look at the palms of Jesus. You can still see the mark where death stung *Him.*

Reality Check

Look up the following verses in your Bible. In the blanks provided, summarize what they say about Christ's victory over death.

Hebrews 2:14,15

Revelation 21:3,4

The Lie to Reject

I reject the lie that I am invincible and immortal, because the Bible tells me that death comes to all people. But I also reject the lie that I should live in the fear of death.

THE TRUTH TO ACCEPT

I accept the truth that Christ has defeated death through His death on the cross and His resurrection. I accept the truth that I will die (unless Jesus returns first), but that death is simply a doorway into an eternity with God through Jesus Christ.

PRAYER FOR TODAY

Dear Lord, I choose today to face the reality that death could come to me at any time You choose. Therefore I want to live each day to the fullest, trusting in Your guidance and power to do so. I thank You that I do not need to fear death because of Christ's victory over the grave. I thank You that I have been set free from him who had the power of death—that is, the devil. And I thank You that I am no longer a slave to the fear of death. I look forward to the day when I will see you face to face in heaven—that day when there will no longer be any death. In the name of the Risen Son, Jesus, I pray. Amen.

TODAY'S BIBLE READING: John 19

FURTHER READING: 1 Corinthians 15 and Hebrews 2

Day 20

A Giant Challenge

Be strong in the Lord and in his mighty power
(Ephesians 6:10 NIV).

This time the "giant" wasn't a nine-foot-tall warrior named Goliath; but a rather small-sized college professor. This time the battleground was not the Valley of Elah but a classroom. And this time the weapon was not a spear with an iron tip weighing 15 pounds, but a piece of chalk that tipped the scales at an ounce or two.

But it was a battle nonetheless, and the young man who felt the call of God to stand up to the giant happened to be named David.

At the beginning of the semester the prof, decked out in his "Jesus is coming back and boy is He ticked off" T-shirt, gave his challenge: He mocked anyone who actually believed in God and the power of prayer. He taunted them and dared any and all comers to stand up to him.

This contest had gone on for years. And every year the results were the same: No one had ever had the guts to take the challenge.

It was a simple test, he would say. On the last day of class before Christmas break, he would hold up a piece of chalk and drop it. Anybody who believed in the power of prayer was invited to come forward and ask God to keep the chalk from breaking when it hit the ground.

The moment David heard the challenge, he went to work. He contacted every Christian he knew to get them praying about this challenge all semester: prayer that he would have the courage to stand up to this mocker, and prayer that God would come through. For some Christians it seemed like David was setting up himself (and God!) for embarrassment.

But David knew better. He knew that this was a spiritual battle that challenged the honor of God. And he also knew that it would take God's power, not his, to pull it off. He had to be strong *in the Lord and in His mighty power.*

Finally the day came. The room was filled with a tense excitement as the professor uttered his challenge one last time. His proud eyes scanned the crowded classroom, expecting no one to come forward. After all, no one had ever come forward before.

But the professor had failed to take one thing into account: He had never had David in his class before.

David rose to his feet and began to walk forward. "I'll pray," he called out as he approached the battle line.

The professor was delighted. "Oh, so we actually have someone here who believes in this outdated practice of prayer! So be it. Pray away. We'll wait until you are done. By the way, what is your name?

"My name is David," he replied, and then prayed a brief but heartfelt prayer of faith.

"Is that it?" the disappointed professor inquired in his mocking voice. He had hoped for a longer performance.

David nodded and waited.

With a great dramatic flair the professor raised the piece

of chalk up over his head and let it fall. Time seemed to freeze as the chalk dropped.

But then a miracle happened: The chalk glanced off the professor's pant leg, bounced onto his tennis shoe, and rolled to the floor. Unbroken.

The crowd laughed. The professor blushed. The Christians cheered, "You did it, David!" And a smiling David simply pointed his index finger up to the sky.[1]

David had learned the secret of spiritual battle, just like the Goliath-slayer of the same name. Be strong *in the Lord and in His mighty power.* Don't even think about fighting the devil in the energy of the flesh. Flesh is Satan's home court (or home battlefield) advantage.

By yourself, in your own strength, you don't stand a chance against the devil. But when you move in the authority you have in Christ and rely on His strength, you can move mountains . . . or giants.

You may be a young or weak Christian. You may think you could never stand up to the devil's lies, temptations, or accusing thoughts. But remember, you have a big God on your side.

Be strong in the Lord and in His mighty power. David was, and he saw God come through. So will you.

Reality Check

What are the giants in your life? In other words, what are the areas in which the devil is trying to control you?

How does the story of David (and King David's defeat of

Goliath in 1 Samuel 17) give you confidence that God is big enough to help you defeat the enemy of your soul?

Look up the following verses in your Bible. In the blanks provided, summarize what they say about God's mighty power at work in and through your life.

Ephesians 3:14-21

Ephesians 5:15-20

The Lie to Reject

I reject the lie that I am inadequate, weak, and utterly helpless to resist the attacks of Satan. I refuse to view myself as simply a teenager who can hope only to somehow hang on until I become more "spiritual."

The Truth to Accept

I accept the truth that God Himself lives in me and that He is undefeated in spiritual battle. I recognize that as I choose to be strong in the Lord and in His mighty power, I can put on the full armor of God and stand up to the enemy.

Prayer for Today

Thank You, Lord, that I can be filled with the Spirit of God and live by His power. I thank You that You are able to do far beyond what I can even ask or imagine, and that Your power dwells in me. I therefore choose to run to the battle lines that come my way today, confident that the God who was with David will also be with me. I believe that the enemy is terrified of the Lord Jesus, and so I put my complete trust in His power to wage spiritual battle today. In Jesus' unbeatable name I pray. Amen.

Today's Bible Reading: John 20

Further Reading: 1 Samuel 14; 1 Samuel 17

Day 21

Pick the Right Fight

Put on the full armor of God, that you may be able to stand firm against the schemes of the devil. For our struggle is not against flesh and blood, but against . . . the world forces of this darkness (Ephesians 6:11,12).

The Dream Team. Talent and giftedness beyond belief, and all on the same team in the same place at the same time! They cruised to the men's basketball gold medal in the 1992 Olympics with awesome style and power.

In 1996 they want to put together another Dream Team. The final choices remain (at this writing) to be seen, but you've got to expect the likes of The Shaq, The Mailman, Hakeem the Dream, and others to be there in Atlanta.

Imagine for a moment that it is the championship game between the United States and, say, Russia. Both teams are going for the gold. Picture this: There are about three minutes left in regulation, and the U.S. team is up by five points.

Suddenly Shaquille O'Neal and Hakeem Olajuwan start to trash talk each other. Shaq had fired a perfect pass to Olajuwan and it bounced off his hands and out of bounds. So Shaq rags him about it, and Hakeem gets upset. The good-natured ribbing quickly turns nasty, and the two are jawing loudly at each other even as the game continues.

Finally it gets to the point where Hakeem angrily drills Shaquille with the ball when he gets the inbound pass. It sails out of bounds. Turnover! The Russian team gets the ball back with 35 seconds to play, down by two.

The U.S. team is so shaken by the angry words and actions of its teammates that they become distracted . . . just for a moment. But that's all it takes. The point guard for the Russian team is sprung loose outside the three-point line, and he nails a 22-footer at the buzzer for the victory.

What happened? The Dream Team became the Nightmare Team. Why? They lost sight of who the real opponent was and ended up losing much more.

Today's Scripture warns us to make sure we are fighting the *real* enemy. Because we can see, hear, and touch other people, and because these people (often other Christians!) can "make" us angry, we can be easily duped into thinking they are the enemy.

And that is exactly what our real enemy wants us to think. For if we spend all our time and energy fighting each other, we'll have nothing left to fight Satan and his forces.

No, people are not the enemy. They may be tools of the enemy, and certainly many of them are victims of the enemy. But Christ came to *save* people, not fight with them.

We've got to realize that the "church," the body of Christ, is the ultimate Dream Team. The talent and giftedness of God's people are beyond belief. With Christ as Head and the rest of the body working together under His direction, the kingdom of light is unbeatable! And the devil knows that full well.

So Satan works hard to divide and conquer. He whispers in our ears lies and hateful thoughts about our brothers and sisters in Christ. He tries to stir up racial prejudice. He attempts to trick us into questioning other people's motives. He tries to plant envious or jealous or critical thoughts in our minds.

This is all part of the devil's schemes. We need to stand firm against him by putting on the full armor of God.

The next time you're tempted to get angry or grow bitter, envious, or resentful of a fellow Christian, remember who we are: We are the *true* Dream Team.

Keep in mind who the real enemy is, and pick the *right* fight in life.

Reality Check

Think about your relationships with those in authority over you (parents, teachers, pastors, and so on). In what ways have you begun to see them as "the enemy"?

Think about your relationships with non-Christians at school, at work, or in your neighborhood. In what ways have you begun to see them as "the enemy"?

Think about your relationships with other Christians from your church, your youth group, or other churches. In what ways have you begun to see them as "the enemy"?

Look up the following verses in your Bible. In the blanks provided, summarize what they say about loving other people instead of fighting against them.

1 Corinthians 13:4-8

Romans 12:16-21

The Lie to Reject

I reject the lie that people are the enemy. I recognize this as a scheme of the devil to get me to fight the wrong battle. I reject the temptation to look down on people from other races, ethnic groups, schools, or churches.

The Truth to Accept

I accept the truth that Christ came to save people's lives, not to destroy them. I accept the truth that my enemy is the devil, and I choose to pick the right fight and to put on the full armor of God so I can stand firm against his schemes.

Prayer for Today

Dear Lord, please forgive me for fighting the wrong battles. I have focused on other people and how they irritate, annoy, anger, or abuse me. In so doing I have forgotten who my real enemy is—the devil—and he has taken advantage of my sin. Teach me, Lord, in the days ahead how to put on Your full armor so that I may stand firm against the schemes of the devil. Make me an instrument of love, truth, and forgiveness to the people around me. In Jesus' name. Amen.

TODAY'S BIBLE READING: John 21

FURTHER READING: Jonah

Day 22

I Wished I'd Stayed in Bed

Put on the full armor of God, so that when the day of evil comes, you may be able to stand your ground, and after you have done everything, to stand (Ephesians 6:13 NIV).

Ever have "one of those days"? Maybe you're having "one of those days" today! You know, the kind where everything goes wrong. The kind where you wish you'd never gotten out of bed.

Job had one of those days. Actually he had a couple of them. And it all started with a conversation between God and Satan. You can read all about it in Job chapter 1. Let me give the story to you in my own words.

"Well, well, well, look who's here! What have you been up to, Satan?" God had commanded all the angels to report in, and the devil had showed up with his pointed tail between his legs.

"Oh, just lookin' around." Satan couldn't even look God in the eye.

"I see. Well, what do you think about my servant, Job? Isn't he an incredible man of God?" God knew just how to push Satan's buttons.

"Well, big deal. Of course he loves You. You pamper him and won't let me get near him. But You just take away all the goodies you give him, and he'll curse You to Your face." His pouting and whining turned to bargaining as he lifted a cunning eye toward God.

"Fine. You've got a deal. Do whatever you want with Job. But don't you dare lay a hand on his body."

The devil was off like a shot. And before many days had passed, Job had a day to end all days, courtesy of the devil. Within minutes the following events were reported to him.

> *A band of terrorists ran off with all his donkeys and oxen (Job had thousands of each). They also murdered all but one of the herdsmen.*
>
> *Lightning struck the sheep herd (he had thousands of these as well) and killed all of them plus all but one of the shepherds.*
>
> *Three raiding parties stole all the camels (thousands again) and slaughtered all but one of the camel herders with swords.*
>
> *A terrible windstorm struck the house where all Job's sons and daughters were partying and they all perished.*

On another day soon after, God gave Satan permission to strike Job's body. That poor man then broke out with painful, itching, oozing boils from the top of his head to the soles of his feet.

The evil day. It usually comes without warning. And when it hits, it's too late to scramble around and try to find your armor. It has to be in place already, or the devil's fiery arrows will hit their targets—your heart and mind.

You may be tempted to let down your spiritual guard when things are going well. But it is simply never safe to take off the armor of God.

Jesus promised that in this world and life tough times—evil days—will come (John 16:33). There is nothing you can do to avoid them. The question is: When the evil days come, and the dust clears after the battle, will you still be standing?

The choice is yours: Do you want to stand firm when the enemy comes in like a flood? Jesus has already overcome the world and He wants to train your hands for battle . . . not just to fight, but to win! Learn to put on the full armor of God. It's not an option, it's a command.

Reality Check

Have you been standing firm lately or have you been falling flat on your face when trials come? Think of some recent examples.

Sometimes we can grow very discouraged when we fall and fail. We may wonder if we'll ever be able to live the Christian life. Have you ever thought that the Christian life works for others but not for you?

How does today's verse encourage you to believe there is hope for victory?

Look up the following verse in your Bible. In the blank provided, summarize what they say about the pain and victory of spiritual battle?

2 Corinthians 6:3-10

The Lie to Reject

I reject the lie that says it is safe to relax spiritually when things are easy or going well. I recognize the tactic of the devil to try to lure me into laziness.

The Truth to Accept

I accept the truth that it is never safe to take off the armor of God. Even when things couldn't be better, I recognize that the evil day could come at any moment. But I also accept the truth that I can stand firm by putting on the full armor of God. Therefore I can live my life in confidence and not fear.

Prayer for Today

Lord, I thank You for the times of rest and refreshment from the battle. I see that those times are for the healing of my body, soul, and spirit so that I can fight again. I want to keep my armor polished and in place. Protect me from spiritual laziness. Even on the good days, help me to keep watching and praying so that I will not enter into temptation. I know that the evil day could come at any time, but I also know that Your armor is enough to protect me. I choose to put on the full armor of God today. In Jesus' name. Amen.

TODAY'S BIBLE READING: Romans 1

FURTHER READING: Romans 13 and Ephesians 6

Day 23

Buckle Up for Safety!

Stand firm then, with the belt of truth buckled around your waist (Ephesians 6:14 NIV).

It's quickie quiz time, and you might be surprised at what you learn! Just circle "T" for "True" or "F" for "False" for each of the following:

1. God helps those who help themselves. T F
2. All religions are basically the same. T F
3. Christians are vulnerable to demonic attack. T F
4. Depression is a physical and mental problem. T F
5. A person has the right to choose to die with dignity if he or she is very old or very sick. T F

Okay, let's see how you did. The answer to number 1 is F. A true statement would be, "God helps those who trust in Him." See John 15:1-8, James 4:6, and Proverbs 3:5,6 for starters.

How about number 2? False again. Jesus said in John 14:6 NIV that He is "the way and the truth and the life." He didn't say He was "a way or a truth." No one comes to the

Father except through Him. Check out Acts 4:12 as well. All other religions are dead ends.

You should realize by now that number 3 is True. First Peter 5:8 warns us that our adversary, the devil, is prowling around like a roaring lion looking for people to devour. The next verse, 1 Peter 5:9 NIV, tells us to "resist him, standing firm in the faith." Obviously, only Christians can stand firm in the faith, so that warning was directed to believers.

Number 4 is a little trickier because it's really a half-truth. Of course depression will affect your body (you might be very tired out or you might have insomnia, for example). And it certainly affects your mind (you may think things are hopeless). But it is also a spiritual problem. Psalm 43:5 NIV gives a spiritual solution for depression: "Why are you downcast, O my soul? Why so disturbed within me? Put your hope in God, for I will yet praise him, my Savior and my God."

Finally, number 5. Does a person have the right to choose to end it all ("die with dignity") if he or she is so old or so sick that he doesn't feel like living anymore? No, he doesn't! Jesus said that He holds the keys of death and Hades (Revelation 1:18)—not Jack Kevorkian or anybody else. We have no more right to choose the time and manner of our death than we did to choose the time and manner of our birth!

So why did we go through all that? To prove a point—that spiritual battle is primarily a battle between truth and lies. Jesus is the truth (John 14:6), God's Word is the truth (John 17:17), and Satan is the father of lies (John 8:44). He is the "god of this world" (2 Corinthians 4:4), and the world is filled with his lies.

If Satan can get you to believe a lie, he can control how you think, feel, and act in that area. You don't believe me? Think about it: Is abortion right? Of course not. But if a pregnant woman believes abortion is morally right and her "right," will it affect how she feels and acts? Of course! She can have her baby killed and probably feel no remorse about it at all.

Having the belt of truth buckled in your life means that you think biblically. You know what the Bible says is true, and you reject anything that contradicts that truth.

But this doesn't come by accident. It comes by study.

Ask God to give you a love for His Word. Pray that He will help you to believe what it says, understand what it means, and obey what it tells you to do.

Buckle up with the belt of truth, God's Word, today. It will help keep you from crashing and burning spiritually.

Reality Check

Do you struggle with getting into the Bible? Do you ever get distracted while reading it and have trouble concentrating? Knowing that the Bible is truth which will set you free (John 8:31,32), can you see why you might be experiencing such a battle?

What are some of the benefits of studying God's Word? (If you are really motivated to find out, read through Psalm 119!)

Look up the following verses in your Bible. In the blanks provided, summarize what they say about the importance of God's Word.

2 Timothy 3:16,17

John 17:15-17

The Lie to Reject

I reject the lie that says I can have a casual attitude toward reading and studying God's Word and still do all right spiritually. I also reject the lie that the Bible is too hard to understand or that it is boring. These are obvious tactics of the enemy to keep me from knowing the truth that will set me free.

The Truth to Accept

I accept the truth that "man does not live on bread alone, but on every word that comes from the mouth of God" (Matthew 4:4 NIV). *God's Word is my spiritual food, and I absolutely need to know it in order to walk with God and win in spiritual battle.*

Prayer for Today

Lord, I have to admit that I have not always seen how important the truth of Your Word is to my life. I confess that many times I have believed the devil's lies and not longed for the pure milk of the Word (1 Peter 2:2,3). *Thank You for forgiving me and for opening my eyes to see the battle that rages around me to keep me bound in the world's lies. I now commit myself to becoming a "workman who does not need to be ashamed and who correctly handles the word of truth"* (2 Timothy 2:15 NIV). *I trust in Your power to enable me to do that. In Jesus' name. Amen.*

Today's Bible Reading: Romans 2

Further Reading: Psalm 119

Day 24

Go for the Gold!

God's laws are pure, eternal, just. They are more desirable than gold (Psalm 19:9,10 TLB).

Gold. The mere mention of the word can get the adrenaline pumping. People drool over it. Women dream of it. Men have killed for it.

Some people have left their jobs to "prospect" full-time. Others belong to prospecting associations and clubs, trying their weekend luck in hopes of striking it rich.

George Massie founded such a group, the Gold Prospectors Association of America, back in the late sixties. A couple years ago George was dredging up riverbed gravel when his equipment struck a huge boulder. He was sure there was gold under that rock, so he started working to move it.

After attaching cables and air-filled 55-gallon drums to the boulder, he was finally able to float it free from its hole. Incredibly, 800 ounces of gold nuggets were sitting under that rock, like eggs under a hen!

George Massie that day "hatched" more than $600,000 worth of gold!

Greenhorns (those new to the prospecting business) can

easily get tricked by iron pyrite, more commonly known as "fool's gold." Fool's gold is also a shiny, gold-colored metal, just like the real thing.

But George Wheeldon, a California geologist, hit the nugget right on the head. Talking about the confusion between real gold and fool's gold, he said, "That usually happens before they see their first real nugget. *Once you've seen the luster of real gold, you won't be fooled by anything else.*"

That is an awesome principle to apply to the Christian life. The more you know what God's Word really says, the less likely you are to fall for the lies of the enemy. And those lies can be very clever.

For example, the Jehovah's Witnesses talk about the need to have faith in Jesus the Son of God. They quote verses from the Bible and pray. They often talk and act like true Christians, but they are not.

How can I say that? Listen closely. They believe that Jesus is *the Son of God*, but they do not believe that He is *God the Son*. They believe that Jesus was at one time created, just as you and I have been. He is "the first and greatest creation of Jehovah God," according to Jehovah's Witnesses.

But the true Christian church has always held to the truth that Jesus has always existed, because He is God! Colossians 2:9 TLB puts it this way: "In Christ there is all of God in a human body."

Many people have been terribly deceived by cults such as the Jehovah's Witnesses, the Mormons, the Unification Church (Moonies), and others. But this should never be the case for a Christian.

We have the pure gold of the Word of God to teach us the truth that sets us free from sin and deception (John 8:31,32). We do not need to get faked out by the spiritual "fool's gold" of false teaching around us.

It's really true: Once you've seen the luster of real gold, you won't be fooled by anything else!

So go for the gold of God's Word! The nuggets of truth you will find there are a treasure far more valuable for life than all the gold in the world.

Reality Check

Look up the following verses in your Bible. In the blanks provided, summarize what they say about the value of God's Word.

Psalm 19:7-11

Colossians 3:16,17

The Lie to Reject

I reject the lie that says it is more important for me to

pursue money and the things I want to buy than it is to pursue God and His Word. I recognize that being distracted from truly knowing the Bible is a dangerous way to live, making me vulnerable to the lies and deceptions of the cults.

The Truth to Accept

I accept the truth that knowing God and His Word are the most important things I can do, and more valuable than all the gold, silver, and precious gems in the world. I recognize that by knowing the Bible well, I will be able to spot spiritual frauds and fakes, and be better prepared to protect myself and others.

Prayer for Today

Lord, it is so easy to get excited about having money, making money, and spending money. Thank You for showing me that Your Word is far more valuable than riches.

I cannot begin to put a price tag on the value of knowing You and walking in the truth. You want me to be free and stay free of the lies and deceptions of the false teachers and cults around me. So, Lord, I ask You to give me a love for You and Your Word that is greater than anything else in my life. In Jesus' name. Amen.

Today's Bible Reading: Romans 3

Further Reading: Isaiah 55 and Hebrews 4

Day 25

Heart Attack

Put on the breastplate of righteousness
(Ephesians 6:14).

Joseph was the first one to the front of the meeting room. To be honest, it was refreshing to see a popular, football-playing jock weep so openly. His tears were flowing freely from the springs of sorrow, relief, and joy... all at the same time.

Confessing his sexual sin with his girlfriend and the emotional and spiritual agony he had been through, Joseph pulled no punches. He had suffered a painful attack on his heart, and he wanted to warn others. In part, here is Joseph's story in his own words:

> *In the summer of 1994 I met this girl, and by the fall we began seeing each other. Eventually we ended up going steady.*
>
> *Everything was going along fine in our relationship until around Thanksgiving, when kissing just wasn't enough. At first we just started messing around (touching) and by Christmas it grew to more than just messing around. We decided that we would never have sex, though (Yeah, right).*

By his own admission, the warning bells were going off all over the place, but Joseph shut out the voice of the Holy Spirit. He was set up for a major heart attack.

> *I thought I could resist sex, but one day I couldn't. It was Saturday, April 1, when we had sex for the first time.*

Somehow the word got out, and Joseph's youth pastor, parents, and brother all told him he needed to break up with the girl. But instead of humbling his heart, he hardened his heart and rebelled even more. His rebellion drove him to even more sexual sin.

But God miraculously intervened in Joseph's life and brought him to the end of himself. During that weekend (when he confessed his sin to the group) he found freedom from his guilt and shame. And he went home and broke off that destructive relationship.

This story, unlike too many others, has a happy ending. Listen in again as Joseph sums it up:

> *Now I am able to face God as a child of God with a clear conscience rather than as a no-good teen who had lost his virginity. God also gave me the freedom and liberty to speak openly about my past with my friends, both saved and non-Christians. Now as I look back . . . I can say only one thing: It sure feels good to be a brand-new man!*

There's always a trade-off when you do business with Satan and sin. He will promise you a few moments of ecstasy in exchange for days and weeks (and sometimes years!) of agony. And it all seems worth it until the devil lowers the boom and blasts you in the heart with guilt and shame.

How can you protect yourself? Put on the "breastplate of righteousness." A Roman soldier in the first century wore a breastplate to protect his chest (heart, lungs, and so on) from the enemy's weapons. So what does it mean to put on the breastplate of *righteousness?* It means at least two critical things:

1. *Realize that* in Christ *you already are righteous. You have been forgiven, cleansed and declared not guilty by virtue of the blood of Jesus and your faith in Him. That is who you really are* (2 Corinthians 5:21; Romans 5:1; Hebrews 10:19-22).

2. *Make the choice each day to live a righteous life by the power of the Holy Spirit. This means "putting on the Lord Jesus" like a suit of armor and making no provision for the flesh in regard to its lusts* (Galatians 5:16,17; Romans 13:12-14).

The first step is a matter of faith—believing that what God says about you is indeed true. The second step is a matter of obedience.

Satan will try to deceive you into thinking the first step is a lie. He will try to seduce you into thinking the second step is not worth it.

But there is no sin worth sacrificing a clean, joyful heart that is right with God. No sin . . . not even sexual sin. Just ask Joseph.

Reality Check

Look up the following verses in your Bible. In the blanks provided, summarize what they say about choosing to live a righteous life.

Colossians 3:1-10

Romans 13:12-14

The Lie to Reject

I reject the lie that I am a hopelessly dirty, rotten, no-good sinner, and that all I can expect in the future is dirty, rotten, no-good sin. I also reject the lie that sin will make me happier than living a righteous life. Sin may gratify for a moment, but doing what's right will satisfy for a lifetime.

The Truth to Accept

I accept the truth that I am the righteousness of God in Christ Jesus and that I can choose to live a righteous life through the power of the Holy Spirit. I know that sin may be fun for the moment, but it carries a burden of guilt, shame, and hardness of heart that will cause great heartache for me and others.

Prayer for Today

Lord, I want to thank You for Your Word, which exposes the lies and deceptions of the devil and shows them for what they are. I recognize that there are strong temptations around me to experiment with sin. I battle with a curiosity that can lure me toward evil. But when I think about Your love for me and the devil's hatred of me, I see sin for what it is: just like a child molester trying to lure a kid into a car with a piece of candy. Sure, the candy may taste good, but the consequences of taking it are horrible. So I choose today to put on the breastplate of righteousness. I put on the Lord Jesus and make no provision for the flesh in regard to its lusts. Amen.

Today's Bible Reading: Romans 4

Further Reading: Colossians 2 and 3

Day 26

Good News Shoes

Your feet fitted with the readiness that comes from the gospel of peace (Ephesians 6:15 NIV).

My friend Daniel and I decided to go where (almost) no white man had gone before—the Hispanic section of a town called Casablanca. Knowing that our presence would attract curiosity, we hoped we could use that interest to tell people about Jesus.

We knew that Casablanca was better known for drug deals and gang shootings than spiritual life, so we prayed hard as we walked down the street.

Hoping to find someone who spoke English, we knocked on the door of a small, tan, ranch-style home. The woman of the house answered and gestured across the street. Her teenage daughter, Maria, who spoke English, was there. Her two younger daughters raced across the street to fetch her.

I'm sure heads must have been peeking out from behind curtains all over the block. And I'm sure Maria was wondering why in the world two white men wanted her.

When she arrived we asked Maria if she was interested in talking about spiritual things. She kind of smiled and shook her head.

"In my church it is a sin to dance," she said a bit angrily.

Out of the corner of my eye I spotted a rosebush with a beautiful yellow rose on it. It was in her front yard, so I motioned for Maria to follow me as I walked toward the bush.

"Maria, the issue is not dancing or not dancing. The issue is: Will you receive Christ as your Savior? Look at this rose. Just as this beautiful flower opened from a bud, so God wants to take your life and make it blossom. Could you trust in a God like that?"

She nodded. After explaining the gospel in more detail I asked if she would like to receive Christ. She said she would.

At my invitation, the three of us kneeled in her front yard. Maria prayed a wonderful prayer to receive the Lord Jesus.

Her little sisters, who were already believers, were jumping up and down for joy. It turned out that Maria's mother and aunt who lived with them were Christians as well! So I told Maria to go inside the house and tell them what she had done.

She came out a few minutes later, describing how her aunt had hugged her and how her mother had said, "This is what we have been waiting for all your life!"

Daniel and I were beside ourselves with joy. We were able to encourage Maria in her faith for awhile, but then we had to leave.

As we started walking away, Maria called after us, "You guys are angels, aren't you?"

I smiled and said, "No, Maria, we *are* God's messengers, but we are people just like you."

We walked on a little farther and she called out again. "I know you guys are angels!"

Daniel and I laughed and thanked God for the chance to tell others about Jesus, who brings life and peace to hurting, needy people.

Are your feet ready to go out and tell others the good news that Jesus wants to save them from sin? Before you can "snatch people out of the fire" (see Jude 23), you need the right "footwear."

The Roman soldier wore sandals that had support straps wrapped around his feet and ankles. On the bottom of those sandals were spikes to give him great traction and mobility.

For you as a Christian, putting on the sandals of the gospel of peace means at least three things:

1. *First, it means you know that you are at peace with God, having been declared not guilty of sin through your faith in the Lord Jesus* (Romans 5:1). *The war is over between you and God! You're on His side now.*

2. *Second, it means casting all anxiety and fear on the Lord in prayer, thanking Him that He'll take care of you. He promises to guard your heart and mind with His peace* (Philippians 4:6,7).

3. *Finally, it means you can go in faith, bringing the good news that God has made peace with mankind through Jesus Christ* (2 Corinthians 5:18-21).

Evangelism is one of the clearest forms of spiritual warfare, because you are storming the gates of hell, seeking to release people from their captivity to sin and Satan. Go for it! Just make sure your shoelaces are tied!

Reality Check

Look up the following verses in your Bible. In the blanks provided, summarize what they say about telling others about Jesus.

1 Peter 3:13-16

2 Timothy 4:1-5

If you aren't sure how to explain the gospel to a non-Christian, ask your youth pastor or youth leader. He or she will be glad to help you.)

The Lie to Reject

I reject the lie that I am not a good enough Christian to tell others about Jesus. I reject all anxiety that would keep me from boldly preaching the gospel, because I am at peace with the God who will protect me.

The Truth to Accept

I accept the truth that I can walk boldly in this world with the sandals of peace in place, because I belong to God. I am an ambassador for Christ and I choose to make Christ my Lord. I choose to cast all anxiety on the Lord in prayer and live a life of thankfulness and peace.

Prayer for Today

Dear Lord, I thank You for the honor of being an ambassador for Christ. I ask for and trust in Your strength to boldly preach the good news (gospel) of Your kingdom. I thank You for Your wonderful peace which will guard my heart and mind as I trust in You and cast every anxiety on You. Guide me today to people who need to hear of the life and peace that are in Jesus.

I want to be used by You to bring others to Christ. May all glory and honor go to You. In Jesus' name I pray. Amen.

Today's Bible Reading: Romans 5

Further Reading: Acts 17 and Acts 26

Day 27

An Impenetrable Shield

In addition to all this, take up the shield of faith, with which you can extinguish all the flaming arrows of the evil one (Ephesians 6:16 NIV).

A Roman soldier was always ready to fight. He was a well-oiled fighting machine whose purpose in life was to enforce Caesar's will. When Paul wrote the passage on spiritual warfare in Ephesians 6, he clearly had the Roman soldier in mind.

Even when temporarily resting from battle, the soldier of Caesar always had the first three pieces of armor in place: the belt, the breastplate, and the sandals. If an enemy attacked suddenly, there would be no time for him to put these pieces on. To be caught dead without them would be to be caught dead!

There is a tremendous truth here for us to remember: *Every day we need to have our minds focused on the truth of God's Word—the truth of who Christ is in us and who we are in Christ.* We need to know that we are forgiven and righteous in God's eyes through Christ and that we are at peace with God. Then, we need to move boldly into each new day committed to walking with God, casting every anxiety on Him and prepared to share the good news of Jesus with those around us.

We too are soldiers of a King. But our King is not Caesar; He is the King of kings! Our purpose in life must be to do our Lord Jesus Christ's will.

We must not become lazy, but always have on the "belt of truth," the "breastplate of righteousness," and the "sandals of the gospel of peace." But those three pieces of armor are not enough. When the enemy attacks, we must quickly pick up our shield.

The Roman soldier's shield was large enough to crouch behind. It was as large as 4 feet high by 2½ feet wide. When his attacker would fire arrows with flaming tar on the tip, the Roman soldier would be safe and secure behind his shield.

The shield of the soldier of Christ is his or her faith. Faith is the ability to focus on God and His Word and trust Him no matter what. And sometimes the "flaming arrows of the evil one" can be very cruel and very vicious.

Sometimes they seem to come from everywhere at once: a painful illness that hits like a ton of bricks. Or one that just won't go away, grinding away our life and energy. Persecution from people we love. Gossip or slander from those who would ruin our reputation. Fear that terrorizes by night or by day. Financial problems that knock the wind out of us or our family. The crushing grief of a broken relationship or death of a loved one. The deep, black holes of depression or loneliness.

In the midst of these onslaughts, the devil sometimes whispers, sometimes shouts to us:

> *Where is your God now?*
> *This is hopeless; there's no way out!*

God must be punishing you.

No one understands. No one cares. You're completely alone.

Go on. Run back to the sins you once did. At least you know there will be some pleasure there.

Would you be able to ward off these fierce attacks if they hit you between the eyes today? You need to be prepared.

Even while at rest, the Roman soldier kept his shield close at hand. He knew he could come under attack at any moment, and being able to lay his hand on his shield instantly was a matter of life and death.

So it is for you and me. Where is your shield of faith today? Do you know your God? Do you know the promises of His Word? When Satan hits you with his best shot (and he will!) will you be groping around for something—anything—to protect you? Or will you take up the shield of faith? God's shield will block every shot of the enemy. It is an impenetrable shield!

Reality Check

Look up the following verses in your Bible. In the blanks provided, summarize what they say about God (and your faith in Him) being a shield.

Psalm 18:1-3

Psalm 28:6-9

The Lie to Reject

I reject the lies of Satan that scream at me when I am in pain, trying to cause me doubt and fear. I reject a sense of hopelessness.

I reject the idea that God is punishing me in anger or that He has abandoned me. I reject the lie that no one else cares or understands what I'm going through. I reject the devil's attempts to isolate me from God and others.

The Truth to Accept

I accept the truth that God is my strength and my shield. He is my rock, my fortress, and my refuge. I accept the truth that He will never leave me nor forsake me. He knows and cares about me and what I'm feeling. Though He may discipline me out of love, He never punishes me out of anger. I realize, too, that others have gone through what I am experiencing and have stood firm (1 Peter 5:9).

Prayer for Today

Dear Lord, thank You for always being there for me. You are the God of all hope, and I refuse to be discouraged even though it looks sometimes like You have abandoned me. I know that You are allowing me to go through tough trials so that my faith will grow. I choose today to stand firm in Your love and power.

I lift up the shield of faith, knowing that You are faithful. Thank You that Your shield will quench every fiery arrow of the devil. Teach me Your truth so that my faith in You will grow stronger for the days of battle to come. In Jesus' name. Amen.

TODAY'S BIBLE READING: Romans 6

FURTHER READING: Psalm 18 and Lamentations 3

DAY 28

Make Sure You're Sure

Take the helmet of salvation (Ephesians 6:17).

"I'm not even sure I believe any of this stuff anymore." Paul shifted uncomfortably in his seat as we prepared to go through the Steps to Freedom in Christ (found in *The Bondage Breaker Youth Edition*).

Paul had received the Lord Jesus as his Savior at about age 12. He had even led some people to Christ during his teen years. But by the time I met with him he had no assurance of salvation. In fact, he said he "had no grounds to enter" into heaven when he died.

Having grown up in a harsh, strict, legalistic church, Paul felt driven to keep a rigid list of spiritual "do's and don'ts." He usually spent five or six nights a week at church, trying somehow to please God.

But he felt like a loser, quitting or failing at everything he tried. And when he felt like God had stopped listening to his cries for help, the spiritual roof fell in on Paul's life.

After falling into sexual sin, Paul rebelled against the whole church scene. He started drinking heavily and dabbled in a smorgasbord of spiritual experiences—from Yoga to transcendental meditation to Zen Buddhism. He even stuck his nose into the dark world of the occult, playing around with palm reading, tarot cards, astrology, "white" magic, and more.

The battle for Paul's mind intensified, and he had a horrible bout with depression. Suicidal pictures popped into his head; he would think about driving his motorcycle 150 miles per hour and crashing it on purpose. Anger and bitterness controlled his thought life as he daydreamed about people he hated being horribly killed.

By the time I met with him, this young man was about as confused spiritually as anyone I'd ever met. But there was a spark of hope within him, and he was desperate to find some relief.

About six hours later, after Paul had confessed and rejected 12 years of spiritual garbage, he was a new man. The life had returned to his eyes and the spark of hope had been fanned into a flame of faith.

"I've not felt this clean in a long time," he told me when we were done. A big grin lit up his face.

That was two years ago. Today Paul is continuing to grow strong in his faith in the face of gut-wrenching pain in his young marriage. But Paul is a different man now. He no longer feels like God has left him. He no longer is driven to somehow please an unpleasable God who is far away in heaven.

Paul knows that God loves him and will never leave him. He has the complete assurance of his salvation, and so he is able to keep on living joyfully when before he would have gone absolutely berserk.

What is the difference? *He has the helmet of salvation firmly in place,* and so Paul is winning the battle for his mind.

How about you? If you were to die tonight, do you know for sure where you would spend eternity? What answer would you give to the Lord if He asked you, "Why should I let you into my heaven?"

If you are not certain that God loves you and has forgiven you completely in Christ, you are a wide-open target for Satan's ruthless attacks: guilt, condemnation, fear of death, a sense of abandonment by God.

God wants you to know for sure that you are saved. Listen to the inspired words of the apostle John:

This is the testimony:

> *God has given us eternal life, and this life is in his Son. He who has the Son has life; he who does not have the Son of God does not have life. I write these things to you who believe in the name of the Son of God so that you may know that you have eternal life* (1 John 5:11-13 NIV).

Have you received the Son of God into your life, trusting in His free gift of salvation? Have you seen that your good works do not save you, but it is only by His grace and mercy? If you can answer yes to these questions, then rejoice... and relax. Put on the helmet of salvation, the certain hope of heaven, and let the assurance of God's love and presence in your life protect your mind.

If you can't answer yes to these questions, then open your heart to Jesus right now. Turn from your sin and turn to Him for forgiveness. Don't wait a moment longer. Make sure you're sure.

Reality Check

Look up the following verses in your Bible. In the blanks

provided, summarize what they say about the assurance of salvation.

John 5:24

1 Thessalonians 5:8,9

The Lie to Reject

I reject the lie that says I can never know for sure that I am saved. I refuse to believe the devil's accusations that I am not good enough, spiritual enough, or religious enough to make it into heaven. I reject all thoughts that God does not love me or that He has abandoned me.

The Truth to Accept

I accept the truth that I am saved by the grace of God through faith in Jesus, and that everyone who has Jesus has eternal life. I believe that nothing can ever separate me from God's love for me in Christ and that He will never leave nor forsake me.

Prayer for Today

Dear Lord, thank You for the assurance of salvation that

I have through Christ. I choose today to put on the helmet of salvation; no matter how tough things get, I know that You are with me. You love me and are protecting me. May the hope of salvation protect my mind from doubt, fear, guilt, and condemnation when the spiritual battle rages around me. I know that one day my trials will be over and I will be resting in the loving arms of my Savior, the Lord Jesus Christ. I look forward to heaven, my real home. In Jesus' name. Amen.

TODAY'S BIBLE READING: Romans 7

FURTHER READING: 1 Peter 1 and 1 John 5

Day 29

Just Say the Word

The sword of the Spirit, which is the word of God
(Ephesians 6:17).

The devil doesn't play fair. He can attack at just about any time of the day or night, even when you are in church! But one of his favorite times to hit us seems to be in that "twilight" time when we are dozing off to sleep.

One night I was lying in bed waiting for my wife, Shirley, to come out of the bathroom and join me. All of a sudden a lustful thought popped into my head. Unfortunately, it was for a woman other than my wife!

Now where in the world had that invasion of my mind come from? From the devil, obviously. He delights in trying to disturb the precious intimacy between husband and wife.

Fortunately, I sniffed out the source of that foul thought real quick, and so I said out loud (but not *too* loud!), "Satan, I command you to leave me in the name of the Lord Jesus. I choose to focus on 'what is true, honorable, right, pure, and lovely.' "

Immediately the thought was gone. *I had exercised my authority in Christ,* telling the enemy where to go. And I quoted a portion of the Word of God—Philippians 4:8, to be exact.

A minute or so later I was still lying in bed waiting for my wife, Shirley, to join me when another thought popped into my head.

"I haven't been a very good Christian this week."

For an instant that statement caught me off guard. I had started a prayer journal a few weeks earlier and had pledged to work on it each day. Unfortunately, a week had gone by and I had not used the prayer journal at all during those seven days.

I started to feel a little guilty and ashamed for my lack of spiritual discipline. My emotions slowly began to sink down into discouragement.

"Wait a minute!" I thought to myself. "I know where that thought came from!"

So again I used my authority in Christ to resist the devil. I said out loud, "Satan I command you to leave my presence, for it is written, 'There is therefore now no condemnation for those who are in Christ Jesus' " (Romans 8:1). The thought instantly left.

I knew the devil was trying to discourage me because the thought in my head was a condemning one. And God does not condemn His children!

It is essential to resist the devil out loud when we are alone and under spiritual attack. Why? Only God can read your thoughts perfectly. Satan cannot know what you are thinking all the time, so he is under no obligation to obey your thoughts.

If there ever was someone who could have resisted the devil with just a thought, it would have been Jesus. But when tempted by Satan in the wilderness, He spoke the Word of God out loud (see Matthew 4). Jesus is our example of how to wage and win spiritual battle. He spoke Scripture to the devil and so should we.

The Word of God is like a sword, slashing the enemy's lies, accusations, and temptations to shreds. That is why you need to know the truth of God's Word. How can you speak the Word of God from your mouth if it is not in your heart?

The spoken Word of God is the major offensive weapon we have in fighting against the assaults of the devil. Satan is not impressed with your forceful personality, your ability to debate or argue, your intelligence, or your vocabulary. Nor is he threatened when you raise your voice and yell at him.

But the devil cannot stand before the truth of the Word of God spoken in the authority of Christ by a child of God who is walking in submission to the Father. The Holy Spirit has supplied the weapon that causes Satan to cringe and tremble in fear. It is the Bible. So when you are attacked, don't be frightened. Just say the Word.

Reality Check

Are you equipped with the truth of God's Word to ward off Satan when he attacks? Here is just a brief sampling of Bible verses that relate to some areas of struggle in oui lives. Pick out a couple that especially apply to you, look them up, and commit them to memory.

Anger: James 1:19,20

Anxiety: Philippians 4:6,7

Bitterness: Ephesians 4:31,32

Depression: Philippians 4:4

Guilt: Romans 8:1

Lust: 2 Timothy 2:22

Pride: James 4:6,7

Rebellion: Colossians 3:20

Fear: 2 Timothy 1:7

Of course, there are many other areas not listed here. Consult your pastor, youth pastor, or other mature Christian friend to help you find Scripture for other areas of life.

The Lie to Reject

I reject the lie that says I can resist the devil with my strong personality, my clever arguments, or my loud voice. This is a battle between truth and lies, and I reject the pride that says I can handle it on my own.

The Truth to Accept

I accept the truth that the Word of God is the sword of the Spirit that will effectively defeat the devil's attacks. I accept the truth that it is my responsibility to learn the Word of God so that I can "pull out the sword" when I come under attack.

Prayer for Today

Dear heavenly Father, thank You for giving me your armor. I see that when every piece is in place I will be able to stand firm against the schemes of the devil. I thank You in particular for the sword of the Spirit, which is the Word of God. Teach me through Your Holy Spirit how to use that sword. Please give me power and discipline to study the Bible and commit it to memory so that the Spirit of God can bring just the right Scripture to my mind at the right time. I thank You for the power of Your spoken Word. In Jesus' name. Amen.

Today's Bible Reading: Romans 8

Further Reading: Jeremiah 23 and 2 Timothy 3

Day 30

Something's Happening!

Pray in the Spirit on all occasions with all kinds of prayers and requests. With this in mind, be alert and always keep on praying for all the saints (Ephesians 6:18 NIV).

Philip was a little scared as he walked down the hall to his principal's office. This junior at a high school in Florida was not nervous because he was in some kind of trouble; he was a bit anxious because he was marching onto the front lines of spiritual battle.

"Can we start using a classroom before school hours to begin a Bible study and prayer group?" Philip asked.

The principal did not think that was a good idea.

But Philip did not back down. He mentioned to the principal that he might have to contact a national organization that protects the Constitutional rights of students. Suddenly the principal felt that the Bible study/prayer group was a very good idea!

Less than two weeks later, 30 students started meeting together in a classroom at that school to study the Bible and pray.[1]

Something's happening!

A group of seven junior high students decided to devote their lunchtime at school to fasting, praying, and witnessing to their friends. Some of them prayed while the rest shared their faith in the lunchroom. On the first day they saw several of "the most unlikely" of their friends receive the Lord!

Something's happening!

From a small movement of prayer in Texas, millions of students around the world now gather once a year around the flagpole at their school in September to pray. "See You at the Pole" is happening!

A thousand-plus youth and youth leaders gave up their usual Labor Day weekend in Philadelphia to pray together for a national revival and awakening among youth in our nation. This conference, sponsored regionally each year by Student Venture, the high school outreach of Campus Crusade for Christ, is called *Something's Happening, USA.*

Indeed, something *is* happening across our nation. It's called *prayer.*

As God's people we have the incredible privilege and opportunity to come into the very presence of the Lord of hosts anytime and anywhere.

Prayer is like the air cover in a war. The ground troops and the artillery and tank divisions are vulnerable to enemy fire unless the Air Force knocks out their weapons. Then, once that is accomplished, the troops can move in and mop up.

In spiritual battle, things are no different. You can have the most wonderful teaching, the most clever evangelistic strategies, and the most gifted people around. But if these are not bathed in prayer, the fruit will be minimal. Yet if prayer is taken seriously, watch what God does!

Today's Scripture says we are to "pray in the Spirit on all occasions." What does this mean? It means you allow the Holy Spirit to set the agenda for your praying. Allow Him to fill you with a spirit of praise and thanksgiving to God as you come before Him (see Psalm 100). Let Him show you what and how and who to pray for.

Romans 8:26 tells us that we don't know how to pray as we should, but that the Holy Spirit helps us pray. So Spirit-led prayer is essential. Prayer that is directed by God the Holy Spirit will most certainly be heard and answered by God the Father!

Don't ever think you are too young in age or spiritual maturity to pray. God delights in the prayers of His people (Proverbs 15:8), no matter who they are. In fact, at the recent General Consultation of World Evangelization (GCOWE) in Seoul, Korea, 50 children (mainly elementary school age!) were flown in from around the world to pray for that event. These were children who were known as genuine intercessors (prayer warriors). I know that heaven was "all ears" when those kids prayed!

So don't miss out on this movement of God. Like a tidal wave racing across the sea, mounting up as it prepares to crash upon the land, so is the Spirit of God moving. And He moves in response to the prayers of His people. There's no doubt about it... something's happening!

Reality Check

Concentrating and staying alert in prayer is a battle. Why do you think the devil so strongly opposes our praying?

What are some things you can do to stay alert in prayer? (For example, praying in a group and praying out loud can help.)

Ask the Lord right now to show you how He wants you to be involved in prayer, individually and with other Christians.

Look up the following verses in your Bible. In the blanks provided, summarize what they say about prayer.

John 14:12-14

1 John 5:14-16

The Lie to Reject

I reject the lie that prayer is a last resort when nothing else works. I recognize that the devil will do anything to hinder me from praying. I also reject any and all efforts of Satan to distract me, detour me, and discourage me from prayer by attacking my mind, for I have the mind of Christ.

The Truth to Accept

I accept the truth that Spirit-led prayer is essential to victory in spiritual battle and fruitfulness in ministry. I recognize that if I abide in Christ and His Word abides in me, I can ask whatever I wish and it will be done for me (John 15:7). *I accept the truth that my prayers are the delight of God.*

Prayer for Today

Dear heavenly Father, I confess that I have only skimmed the surface of the mighty, deep ocean of prayer. Lord, teach me to pray. Open my eyes to Your incredible resources which can only be tapped by prayer. Please direct me to other people who have a burden for prayer so that together we can see our families, schools, churches, communities, country, and world touched by You, Almighty God. My spirit is willing, but my flesh is weak. Strengthen me by Your Holy Spirit to pray. I choose to allow the Spirit to direct my praying in every way. In the mighty name of Jesus I pray. Amen.

Today's Bible Reading: Romans 9

Further Reading: Luke 11 and John 17

Day 31

The Lure of Darkness

When men tell you to consult mediums and spiritists, who whisper and mutter, should not a people inquire of their God? Why consult the dead on behalf of the living? To the law and to the testimony! If they do not speak according to this word, they have no light of dawn (Isaiah 8:19,20 NIV).

What is dark and mysterious is "cool." What is evil is "in." What is gory and grotesque is fascinating. That is how many young people feel today. And that's scary.

There is a lure of secret knowledge and special power that entraps many young people in the world of the occult. Dabblers, experimenters, and Satanist wanna-be's can easily become trapped in the snares of Satan. Some end up becoming dupes (or worse) for hard-core Satanists.

I (Neil) once counseled the victim of a medium (channeler). Rory, a sharp-looking man in his late forties who had just gone through a divorce, came into my office and told me his incredible story.

One day he had taken a date named Bernice to an amusement park. While they were walking through the shops they came to a little store advertising a resident psychic. The sign read: "Come in and receive instructions for your life."

Rory and Bernice went inside, and the psychic amazed them with her knowledge about secret things. Whether she was a true medium receiving information from a familiar spirit (demon) or was just a clever con artist, I don't know. But the effect on the couple was deep and powerful.

"If you have this kind of power," Rory exclaimed, "what else can you do for me?"

The psychic promised she could help him become a success in his job and in all other areas of life.

Rory fell for it, and he and Bernice began seeing the psychic regularly. One of the woman's first pieces of advice was that the couple should marry, which they did. As husband and wife, the two continued to follow the psychic's advice on other areas of life.

Almost four years later Rory was in my office. His marriage to Bernice was a disaster, and the job which the woman had promised would be so successful was a bust.

When I asked him how much money he had poured down the drain in his pursuit of "spiritual" knowledge, Rory answered, "I personally gave her almost $15,000, but Bernice lost over $65,000."[1]

Mediums. Spiritists. Channelers. Ouija boards. Magic Eight balls. Tarot cards. Crystal balls. Horoscopes. New Age. White magic. Black magic. Witchcraft. Satanism. There is an almost endless variety of occult practices that promise knowledge and power—to control illness, finances, relationships, the future.

But as Isaiah said, "Should not a people inquire of their God?" In other words, why consult a hateful, evil demonic force when you can gain wisdom from the God of the universe who loves you? Why join forces with a defeated angel (Satan) when you can be in the presence of the King of all kings, the Lord Jesus Christ?

Why settle for rotten meat when you can have prime rib? It is utter stupidity to settle for the devil's corrupt counterfeits when you can have the genuine article, the real thing!

Sure, the devil has a little power and a little knowledge. But compared to our Almighty, all-knowing Father, he's nothing.

Isaiah is right: "To the law and to the testimony [the Word of God]! If they do not speak according to this word, they have no light of dawn" (NIV). The lure of darkness is real, but don't get sucked into that trap. There is only heartbreak, suffering, and death at the end of that road. Choose instead to look for the light of dawn. It is the light of truth and life. It is the light of Jesus.

Reality Check

Look up the following verses in your Bible. In the blanks provided, summarize what they say about the occult.

Deuteronomy 18:9-13

Acts 13:8-12

The Lie to Reject

I reject the lure of darkness and the enticing mystery of the occult which promise secret knowledge and power for life. I recognize this as a deception, because Satan only seeks to trap, control, and devour those who enter his lair. I reject the lie that says thrills and excitement without regret await me in the occult.

The Truth to Accept

I accept the truth that God and His Word are the light of dawn for my life. I recognize that God has all power and all knowledge and the devil is not even close. I accept the truth that Christ came to give me life to the fullest, but the devil brings only bondage and death.

Prayer for Today

Dear Lord, I confess that I have sometimes been curious or fascinated by the world of the occult. Yet now I see that all of these demonic beliefs and practices are an abomination to You. I turn away from any interest at all in the unfruitful deeds of darkness. Open my eyes to see, Lord, any way in which I have been deceived. Show me if I am involved in anything that is of the devil—including the music I listen to, the movies I watch, or the material I read.

I choose today to walk in the light of God and truth. In Jesus' name. Amen.

Today's Bible Reading: Romans 10

Further Reading: Isaiah 47 and Acts 13

Day 32

Tailor-Made Temptation

Do not love the world or anything in the world. If anyone loves the world, the love of the Father is not in him. For everything in the world—the cravings of sinful man, the lust of his eyes and the boasting of what he has and does—comes not from the Father but from the world (1 John 2:15,16 NIV).

Jesus must have been exhausted. He had been led by the Holy Spirit into the wilderness to go one-on-one with the devil. The Bible says that after 40 days and nights of fasting, Jesus became hungry (Matthew 4:2).

Now we're not talking about a few minor hunger pangs here. Jesus needed to eat or He would die. Spiritually vigorous but physically weakened, Jesus was cruelly tempted by Satan. The devil hit Him with his best shots. Let me put that battle into my own words, based on Matthew 4:3-11:

Satan, the master tempter, slithered up alongside Jesus and said, "Listen, big shot, since you're God's Son, you can do whatever you want. You're hungry, so why don't you just turn one of these rocks into a loaf of warm, fresh-baked bread? After all, enough is enough with this fasting business."

Jesus replied, "The Bible says that 'man does not live on bread alone, but on every word that comes from the mouth of God.' " In other words, Satan, my Father's Word is what I live by, not my gut. He will tell me when to eat again, not you and not even me.

So the devil took Jesus back to Jerusalem and had Him perch way up high on the top of the temple roof. "Okay, but what about this idea? After all, if you are the Son of God, why not do a swan dive off this roof, for the Bible says, 'He will command his angels concerning you, and they will lift you up in their hands, so that you will not strike your foot against a stone.' Go ahead, Jesus—the crowds will love it, and the Bible says it's okay."

Jesus said to him, "Nice try there, Satan, twisting God's Word like that. But the Bible also says, 'Do not put the Lord your God to the test.' I refuse to force my Father to save me."

The devil had only one more idea, so he took Jesus on a vision trip, showing him all the world's kingdoms and their wealth and glory. "Listen, Jesus, I'll make you a deal. All the world is under my command. I'll gladly trade it to you if you will just worship me. Just once. Just for a moment. And then I'll be happy and you'll be king of the world!"

Jesus scowled at Satan with eyes of fierce anger and said with a voice that could level a mountain, "Get out of my sight, Satan! For the Bible says, 'Worship the Lord your God, and serve him only.' "

Then the devil fled for his life, and angels came to encourage Jesus.

Jesus was tempted, make no doubt about it. But He never sinned, because He would not fall for the temptations of the devil.

But did you notice *how* the devil tempted our Lord? He tempted Him to turn a rock into bread, to jump off the temple, and to worship him (Satan). When was the last time you were tempted in those three areas?

You see, the devil tailor-makes his temptations for you and me. He knows our areas of weakness, so he cooks up just the right dish, hoping we will sniff the scent and bite on the bait.

John says that temptation comes in three main categories—our fleshly cravings (such as immoral sex, eating too much, sleeping too much, drunkenness, getting high, anger, quarrels, violence, and so on), the lust of the eyes (greedily wanting and envying things we don't have), and the boasting of what we own and what we have accomplished.

What are your areas of weakness? Realize that the devil knows what they are and is constantly trying to set you up to fall in those areas.

The solution? Don't love the things of the world. Love God instead. Don't try to fill up the empty spots in your life and don't try to meet your needs by yourself. Trust God to take care of you in His own time and in His own way. He is faithful.

And when the devil's temptations hit, do like Jesus did: Give the devil the Word of God right between the eyes. Once he has fired all his shots and watched them fizzle at your feet, he'll run for his life. He did with Jesus, and he'll do the same with you.

Reality Check

God has created us with legitimate needs that He wants to meet in His own time and in His own way. When we take matters into our own hands, however, we can fall into temptation. Look at the following list and ask God to show you how you may be falling into the flesh. Then confess those areas to God and turn away from your own ways.

The first item is your real need; the second is a sin of the flesh:

physical rest vs. *laziness*

quietness vs. *fearful shyness*

hard work vs. *workaholism*

excellence vs. *perfectionism*

self-respect vs. *conceit*

communication vs. *gossip*

affection vs. *sexual immorality*

eating vs. *gluttony*

discipline vs. *over-control*

cautiousness vs. *unbelief*

generosity vs. *wastefulness*

friendship vs. *homosexuality*

enjoying life vs. *sensuality and excess*[1]

The Lie to Reject

I reject the lying temptation to doubt that God will take care of me and meet my needs. I reject every slanderous attack by the devil against God's faithfulness, goodness, power, and love.

The Truth to Accept

I accept the truth that I have real needs and that my heavenly Father will always be faithful to meet those real needs in His own way and in His own time. I realize that to be tempted is not the same thing as committing a sin. Jesus was tempted in all things as we are, yet was without sin.

Prayer for Today

Dear Lord, I thank You for Jesus, who understands what it is like to be tempted. I thank You, too, that since He defeated every temptation that came to Him, He can show me the path to freedom and victory. I thank You also for the real needs that You have created in me. May they be constant reminders of my need for You. Help me to distinguish between things I really need and things I only want. And give me patience through the Holy Spirit to wait on Your perfect timing to meet my needs. In Jesus' name. Amen.

Today's Bible Reading: Romans 11

Further Reading: Matthew 4 and Luke 4

Day 33

Way Out!

No temptation has seized you except what is common to man. And God is faithful; he will not let you be tempted beyond what you can bear. But when you are tempted, he will also provide a way out so that you can stand up under it (1 Corinthians 10:13 NIV).

To eat or not to eat. For most people this is not a big issue. True, they may overeat a bit or indulge too much in fatty, salty, or sugary foods, but for them eating is just an enjoyable part of life.

Not so for others. For an increasing number of young people, food is an obsession. All day long they think about avoiding food or are severely tempted to binge (gorge themselves), usually followed by purging (vomiting, taking laxatives, and so on).

Often accompanied by a compulsion to constantly exercise and a fixation on calories, anorexia nervosa is a spiritual bondage that can kill. It is "dieting gone wild." And the trauma to the body caused by bulimia (bingeing and purging) can be deadly as well.

Either way, eating disorders are a life-or-death battle for the mind. Usually they start with a voice in the head saying something like:

You don't need to eat that.

or

If you eat that, you're going to be fat.

or

Go ahead, eat that. It'll make you feel better.

followed by

Look what you did! You're going to get fat!

or

Things are out of control around you;
at least you can control your eating.

The temptation to listen to and follow the cruel "advice" of the devil's voice in our minds can seem overwhelming. But no matter how intense and persistent he is, there is good news: *You do not have to give in.*

Today's Scripture says that God will never allow you to be tempted to the point where you *have* to sin. He will always provide a way out, an escape hatch to endure the temptation.

For freedom to become a consistent reality, you must deal with the root issues in your life, such as fear, insecurity, control, and perfectionism. These must be renounced and replaced by the truth of God's Word.

But the bottom line is that you must recognize where the tempting voice is coming from: the devil. And you must stand on your authority in Christ against him. Commit your body and mind to the Lord Jesus and command Satan to leave you in His name.

Can victory over eating disorders (and other severe temptations that torment our minds) be a reality? Listen to this letter and rejoice:

Dear Neil,

I can't begin to tell you all that the Lord has done in my life through the truth you shared with us at the conference. I am now more aware of the deception of the enemy, and this makes my gratefulness for my powerful and gracious Savior real. I was bulimic for 11 years, but now I can be in the house alone all day with a kitchen full of food and be in peace.

When a temptation or lie from Satan pops into my mind, I fend it off quickly with the truth. I used to be in bondage to those lies for hours and hours each day, always fearing food. Now I'm rejoicing in the freedom which the truth brings.

No matter how rough the battle, there is hope in Jesus. Don't keep your struggle to yourself. You may feel guilty or ashamed about your problems, but God has His warm, loving heart and arms all around you through the body of Christ (other Christians). They can strengthen you with their prayers and encouragement. You need their help.

Finally, remember that no matter how hard the devil tries to convince you that you are a hopeless case, different from anyone else, he's a liar. The truth will set you free. Jesus will set you free. He'll lead you to the way out.

Reality Check

Look up the following verses in your Bible. In the blanks provided, summarize what they say about overcoming temptation and sin.

Hebrews 2:17,18

Hebrews 3:12,13

The Lie to Reject

I reject the lie that says there is no way out of my bondage and sin. I reject the lie that I have to listen to the voice of the enemy in my head and do his will. No matter how long and hard he persists, I know that I have the mind of Christ and that Jesus is my master, not Satan.

The Truth to Accept

I accept the truth that there is a battle going on for my mind, but that God's Word promises me a way out. I choose to take that way out by submitting my body and mind to God, and by resisting the devil and his lying temptations.

Prayer for Today

My gracious Father, I thank You that Your Word is true, whether I believe it's true or feel it's true. Sometimes the nagging voice of the enemy seems more real, but I know that is part of the deception. I thank You that Satan is a defeated foe and that I belong to the Victor, the Lord Jesus.

I ask You to destroy any and every stronghold in my life that gives the devil ground to attack me. I invite

You to reveal to me all the lies I have believed so that I can confess my unbelief to You and submit every area of my life to You.

I know that as I do this, I can resist the devil in the name of Jesus and he will flee from me. In Jesus' mighty name. Amen.

TODAY'S BIBLE READING: Romans 12

FURTHER READING: Hebrews 4 and James 1

Day 34

The One-Two Punch

Who will bring any charge against those whom God has chosen? It is God who justifies. Who is he that condemns? Christ Jesus, who died—more than that, who was raised to life—is at the right hand of God and is also interceding for us (Romans 8:33,34 NIV).

My pastor, Mike, was once a missionary to Mexico. During his time there he came to know the ways of Mexican police officers, some of which were not too honest. In fact, Mike would often be pulled over while driving and be accused of some false traffic violation. What the policemen wanted was a little "under the table" money to buy some *cerveza* (beer).

Once Mike was riding with one of his friends who owned a powder-blue minivan (a sure tip-off to the Mexican police that they were dealing with an American). They approached an intersection at which the traffic light was stuck on red.

As they slowed to a halt, a police officer on the other side of the intersection waved them on through. So Mike's friend hit the gas and proceeded on through the red light.

You can probably guess what happened next. The traffic cop waved Mike's friend over to the curb and ticketed him for running a red light!

Pretty stinky, huh? Well, Mike thought so, too, so he decided to take some action to protect himself. He happened to be good friends with a man high up in the government. José (not his real name) was not the kind of guy you mess around with. In fact, he was best known for being the chief "spy" for the government.

One day Mike was explaining to José the problems he was having with the traffic cops.

"No problem," José replied; "let me give you my business card. The next time one of those crooked cops pulls you over, just flash my business card and see what happens."

Mike smiled and went on his way, eager to try out José's card. He didn't have to wait long. He was soon pulled over for some bogus reason, but this time Mike was prepared.

"Excuse me, officer, but I was instructed by the owner of this card to show it to you. He thought you might reconsider this ticket." Mike was grinning from ear to ear.

The officer's face went white. "I'm sorry, sir. Move along."

Mike used that card often and had no more problems with false accusations!

Our enemy, the devil, works kind of like the traffic cop at the red light. He tempts us to break God's law. He whispers things such as, "Aw, c'mon, nobody will notice. Once won't hurt. Everybody's doing it." And then once you give in to the temptation you'll hear, "You dirty, rotten, no-good halo-head! You call yourself a Christian? Look what you did!"

It's the old one-two punch: temptation followed by accusation.

Accusation is Satan's attempt to heap guilt and shame upon us; he tries to make us feel unforgiven, unworthy, and unloved by God. And he is very good at it.

What is the solution? Remember that Satan, not the Father, is the one who brings a charge against God's chosen children. We have been declared not guilty (justified) by faith in Christ. The devil, not the Lord, tries to condemn us. Therefore those accusing thoughts are from Satan, not God.

So when the devil appears, pull out your "I Mean Business" card and show it to him. Remind him of who died for you, who was raised from the dead for you, and who sits at the right hand of Almighty God, praying for you. The devil will turn white with fright and say to you, "Move along."

Know the truth of who you are in Christ and exercise your authority in Christ, and you should have few problems with the devil's accusations.

Reality Check

On the next page are listed some of the most common names the devil calls us to make us feel guilty and ashamed. Next to each is a Scripture verse that refutes his accusation. Look up the Bible verses and then memorize one that is particularly helpful to you.

Dirty: John 15:3

Guilty: Romans 5:1

Helpless: Philippians 4:13

Inadequate: 2 Corinthians 3:5,6

Rejected: Jeremiah 31:3

Stupid: 1 Corinthians 2:16

Ugly: Psalm 139:14

Worthless: Ephesians 2:10

The Lie to Reject

I reject all condemning, accusing thoughts that try to make me feel guilty, dirty, shameful, worthless, or helpless. I recognize that they come from Satan, the father of lies.

The Truth to Accept

I accept the truth that God has forgiven me, declared me "not guilty," and cleansed me by virtue of the blood of Jesus and my faith in Him. I declare that I am adequate and competent in Christ to do all that God asks of me, through the power of the Holy Spirit.

Prayer for Today

Dear heavenly Father, I thank You for Jesus. I thank You that He died for my sins, rose from the dead to give me life, and now sits at Your right hand praying for me. I thank You that You will never condemn me for my sins, because "there is therefore now no condemnation for those who are in Christ Jesus" (Romans 8:1). *Strengthen me today to know Your love and to truly believe that what You say about me is true. I realize that listening to the devil's lies will only bring despair, so I choose today to renew my mind with Your living Word.*

In the name of Jesus, who is the way and the truth and the life, I pray. Amen.

TODAY'S BIBLE READING: Romans 13

FURTHER READING: Psalm 44 and Zechariah 3

Day 35

No Regrets

Godly sorrow brings repentance that leads to salvation and leaves no regret, but worldly sorrow brings death (2 Corinthians 7:10 NIV).

Is it God speaking to me? Is it the devil? Or am I just talking to myself? It can get downright confusing at times, and in fact we have devoted a whole book to that subject, *Know Light, No Fear.*

But one thing is certain: We need to be able to distinguish between the *conviction* of the Holy Spirit and the *condemnation* of the devil. If we don't, we will experience major confusion and even despair. The following story is a classic example.

I (Neil) met Alyce after I spoke at a Sunday evening service at a church in San Diego. Alyce was one of the most pathetic-looking young women I have ever met. She was so skinny that she literally had no more body fat to lose. She had lost her job three days earlier, and her vacant eyes showed that she had lost all hope for her life.

Alyce's father told me she had suffered terribly from PMS during adolescence and had become addicted to prescription painkillers. She was a very talented girl and a committed Christian in many ways, but she was also a

Darvon junkie who had even been arrested once for illegal possession of prescription drugs.

As her father told me her sad story, Alyce sat nodding to herself as if to say, "Yes, that's me, and life is the pits."

Finally I turned to Alyce, took her by the hands, and said, "I want you to tell me who you think you are."

"I'm just a no-good failure," she whimpered.

"You're not a failure," I responded. "You're a child of God."

At first the truth did not sink in. She continued to pour out the negative self-talk born out of the devil's cruel accusations. I continued to counter the lies with the good news of her identity in Christ. And the more we talked the more aware I became of Christ's presence encouraging Alyce.

Then the light broke through. "Do you mean to tell me that all these negative thoughts about myself are nothing but satanic deception?" Alyce asked.

"That's right, Alyce," I nodded. "And as you begin to learn the truth about your identity in Christ, you will be free from the bondage of Satan's lies."

Two weeks later Alyce enrolled in an intensive 12-week live-in spiritual growth course in the mountains near San Diego. At the end of that course she began to take initiative in her life instead of remaining the victim of Satan's accusations and deception. She got a job and gained about 25 pounds. Today she's free.[1]

So many Christians live defeated lives like Alyce. Believing that God has given up on them, they give up on themselves. Maybe you can relate.

Do you think God sees you as a failure? Is He fed up with having to keep forgiving you for the same sins over and over again? Is He sick and tired of all your doubts, fears, worries, and depression? Do you see Him as frowning at you, shaking His head in disapproval? Is He saying, "Shape up or ship out!"?

If you answered yes to any of those questions, you have listened to the devil's lies, just like Alyce.

When the Spirit of God convicts you of sin, it is with a gentle but firm voice. He points out *specifically* what you have done wrong, kindly leading you to turn away from that sin (repent) and turn back to your always-loving Father. The Bible calls this convicting work of the Spirit *godly sorrow.* After repentance you feel relieved and restored.

When Satan accuses you, however, it is harsh, condemning, and belittling. You feel like dirt, and there is no relief from his cruel nagging. You are filled with regrets, and you find yourself moaning, "If only I had done this . . . or "If only I had not done that. . . ." And so you end up torturing yourself with the devil's whip at your back.

Can you see the difference between how the devil works and how the Spirit of God works? With the devil there is no relief. With the Lord there are no regrets!

Reality Check

Look up the following verses in your Bible. In the blanks provided, summarize what they say about godly sorrow and repentance.

2 Corinthians 7:11

Romans 2:4

The Lie to Reject

I reject any and all attempts of Satan to mimic the voice of God in my life. I reject the lie that God is tired of me, impatient, and fed up with my failures. I recognize that the devil is lying to me to try and get me to swallow a false view of God and myself and therefore lose hope.

The Truth to Accept

I accept the truth that God is gracious and merciful, slow to anger and full of lovingkindness and truth. I believe that God is kind and that it is His kindness that leads me to repentance. I accept only the godly sorrow that produces repentance without regret.

Prayer for Today

I thank You, Lord, that I don't have to live in slavery to the "if only" syndrome. I thank You that I can leave all my past sins and failures at the foot of the cross. I don't want to wallow in the muck of regret any longer. Thank You for the freedom of knowing that You don't hold these things against me anymore. Please help me to forgive myself as well. I need Your discernment in order to foil the devil's future attempts at accusing me and bringing me down. I thank You that the Spirit of truth will lead me into all truth. In Jesus' name. Amen.

Today's Bible Reading: Romans 14

Further Reading: John 16 and 2 Corinthians 7

Day 36

Put Them to the Test

Do not believe every spirit, but test the spirits to see whether they are from God, because many false prophets have gone out into the world (1 John 4:1 NIV).

Joan was studying at a junior college in the South, and part of her course load was a psychology class. She was halfway through the semester and doing quite well when her teacher started to show her true colors.

One Friday the professor asked the class to close their eyes as she began to speak to them about deep-breathing and relaxing. Soon she had the class "visualizing" being lifted up into a crystal-clear, sunny sky and then "flying away."

Next they were told to "drop" onto a sandy beach, take off their shoes, and feel the warmth of the sand. Joan could literally "feel" the heat from the sand.

The class was then led deeper into a form of hypnosis. The students were told to bend their heads down and receive a necklace that would give them incredible power. As she did so, Joan felt incredibly burdened and heavy.

She was then led on a walk through a lush, tropical

scene, but all the time she kept looking over her shoulder because she felt as though she were being followed.

Being guided to walk into a pond, Joan was "feeling" the water when the bell rang for the class to end. She got up and left, suffering from a headache and feeling a bit groggy.

All the next day she had a pounding headache. Then came Sunday. Joan skipped Sunday school but went to the worship service and slid into the pew next to her mom. As the praise music began, she turned to her mother and practically spit on her.

Wildly Joan proclaimed, "I've got to get out of here!" And she did.

When she finally returned home later that afternoon, a godly man prayed for her to be set free. Her headache was instantly gone, and she felt much better. She then realized that it had been Jesus following her during her "travel."

Joan had been a Christian for quite some time and knew the Word of God fairly well. But now she realized she had been deceived and needed to get out of that class.

The professor was astonished. Why would this honor student want to drop out of her class? Joan explained that she objected to being hypnotized and that she wanted no part of that anymore.

The woman tried to touch Joan (something Joan was warned against), but she managed to avoid her. The professor became more and more angry and aggressive, refusing to sign the document releasing Joan from the class.

Finally Joan told her teacher that she believed she was a witch, and that Joan as a Christian could not associate with her. The woman acted shocked and then lunged toward Joan. Boldly Joan told her that she was covered by the blood of Christ and commanded her to leave her alone.

The professor was knocked against the wall . . . stunned. With that she ripped the document from Joan's hand, signed it, shoved it back to her, and told her never to come back again.

Joan learned the hard way that many false prophets have gone out into the world. They may seem harmless, even helpful, but they are wolves in sheep's clothing. They are deceivers.

We need to be on the alert. Not everything spiritual is from God. Not everyone who talks about God, prayer, the Bible, or even Jesus is from God.

Satan's greatest weapon is *deception*. Deception is making something evil look good, or making something good look evil. It can get downright confusing.

And that's why we need to pray that the Holy Spirit will give us discernment. You see, when you are tempted, you know it. When you are being accused, you can see what's what's happening. But when you are being deceived, you're clueless (otherwise you wouldn't be deceived!). But the Spirit of God can help us see through the devil's lies.

So don't believe every spirit, but put them to the "Jesus test." Do they believe that Jesus is the Christ, the Son of God, and God the Son? And do they bow to Him as their only Lord and Savior?

If they say yes, and their lives back up what they say, they pass. If they say no, they flunk. Have no more to do with them.

Reality Check

Look up the following verses in your Bible. In the blanks provided, summarize what they say about deception.

Deuteronomy 13:1-4

Matthew 7:21-23

THE LIE TO REJECT

I reject the lie that says every spiritual experience, vision, teaching, or "gift" that comes my way is from God. I reject the lie that there is an automatic, passive protection for the believer against Satan's deception. I recognize that the devil wants to lure me into a state of complacency.

THE TRUTH TO ACCEPT

I accept the truth of God's Word that commands me to not believe every spirit, but to test the spirits to see if they are from God. I realize that there are many false prophets and deceivers and that I need to be spiritually alert and discerning to avoid their traps.

PRAYER FOR TODAY

Dear heavenly Father, I thank You that nothing is hidden from Your sight. All things are open to You. Please give me Your discernment to distinguish between right and wrong, good and evil. I ask you to teach me how to be more sensitive to Your Spirit's guidance, so that I won't passively accept everything "spiritual" that comes my way. If I have been deceived in any way by a deceiving spirit or false prophet, please reveal that to my mind so I may renounce any and all lies that I have believed. In Jesus' name. Amen.

TODAY'S BIBLE READING: Romans 15

FURTHER READING: Matthew 7 and 2 Peter 2

Day 37

A Devil in Disguise

Satan himself masquerades as an angel of light. It is not surprising, then, if his servants masquerade as servants of righteousness. Their end will be what their actions deserve (2 Corinthians 11:14,15 NIV).

"Why are you carrying the phone around, John?" his mom asked, kind of puzzled.

"Because Uncle Bill and Aunt Theresa are going to call any minute," John answered confidently.

"How do you know that?" John's mom was smiling, amused at the game her 14-year-old son was playing.

But it wasn't a game. Moments later the phone rang, and it was indeed John's aunt and uncle.

John soon after developed the ability to know secret habits of people, even after meeting them only once. Years later his parents would remark to each other and ask him, "How did you know?"

After he learned how to drive, the same voice inside his mind would tell John where the speed traps were.

Though the voice in John's head told him the truth 90 percent of the time, it was not always kind to him. Sometimes it would tell him to burn his arms with a soldering iron or to poke out his eye with a screwdriver. Later in life, while repairing antennas on a hundred-foot radio tower, the voice told him to jump off.

The majority of the time, however, the advice John received was practical and helpful. Even when the voice said he was stupid, ugly, dumb, fat, and therefore would never amount to anything, John still wondered if it was God speaking to him.

Having spent a term on the mission field in Africa as a pilot, John was a sincere Christian with a genuine heart to serve God. But by the time I met him, he was a defeated man. He was tormented by an increasing fear that eventually completely paralyzed him. His wife, too, was suffering. She had spiraled into a black hole of depression, feeling powerless against the spiritual enemies around her.

The day before I took John through the Steps to Freedom in Christ, God revealed to him the root of his problems. For four years he had gone to sleep at night listening to the CBS Radio Mystery Theater. During that time a demonic spirit of fear had gained access to his life, masquerading as a helpful friend.

After a major battle, John was able to renounce that spirit guide and it left him. He was truly set free from the power of darkness that had disguised itself as an angel of light.

When I saw John several months later, it was clear that he was a new man. Faith had replaced fear. Joy had overcome despair. In fact, John had gone back to Africa to collect his belongings, and he said he had received more ministry in those two weeks than in the four years he was previously stationed there! People were so amazed at the change in his life that he often shared his testimony until two or three in the morning.

John's story can be echoed by an increasing number of people who are being duped by the devil in disguise.

Knowing that most people are not interested in being influenced or controlled by a demon, Satan and his cohorts put on a mask. They often literally appear as an angel, offering companionship and advice to the gullible.

Beware of any spirit being that seeks to develop an ongoing relationship with you or someone you know. This is especially true if they give their name(s). Angels in the Bible never developed long-term friendships with people; they came with a message from God and then were gone.

In addition, the only angel who gave his *own* name in the Bible was Gabriel. He identified himself to the priest, Zechariah, the father of John the Baptist, while he was in the holy of holies of the temple.

So be on the alert. The devil delights in disguising himself as an angel of light and even as the voice of God Himself. But he wants to drive you, control you, and jerk you around. Don't listen to him. Learn to tune in only to the gentle, loving guidance of the Spirit of God. There is a world of difference!

Reality Check

Look up the following verses in your Bible. In the blanks

provided, summarize what they say about following the guidance of God.

John 10:2-5 (the shepherd is Jesus and the sheep are His people)

Romans 8:13-16

The Lie to Reject

I reject any and all demonic spirit guides that have been assigned to me or which may be trying to gain access to my mind. I reject the lie that I need any other guidance in my life apart from that which God Himself sends.

The Truth to Accept

I accept the truth that the guidance of the Spirit of truth is what I need and what I want in my life. I accept only the wisdom that comes from above and which is "pure, then peaceable, gentle, reasonable, full of mercy and good fruits, unwavering, without hypocrisy" (James 3:17).

PRAYER FOR TODAY

Most gracious Father, I thank You that You love me enough to give me the wisdom and guidance that I need. I don't want to listen to any spirits masquerading as angels of light. Give me the diligence and perseverance to study Your Word under the direction of the Holy Spirit so that I might be filled with Your wisdom. Teach me to be still and know that You are God so that when You want to guide and lead me I will be quiet enough to hear the Shepherd's voice. In Jesus' name. Amen.

TODAY'S BIBLE READING: Romans 16

FURTHER READING: John 10 and 2 Corinthians 11

Day 38

Snakes Alive!

The Spirit explicitly says that in later times some will fall away from the faith, paying attention to deceitful spirits and doctrines of demons (1 Timothy 4:1).

"Did they tell you about the snakes?" a neighbor asked my friends, Dawson and Karen, as they moved into their "new" house.

"No," they replied, a bit puzzled by what the neighbor meant. It didn't take them long to find out.

"There's a snake upstairs in the bathroom!" The cry went up from one of their kids. And suddenly the hunt was on.

Where were the snakes coming from? The answer to that question proved to be far more complex than the Grover family ever imagined.

Dawson poked around in the basement, and after a lot of searching he discovered the secret: Their washing machine drain led down into a nearby swamp, and every time they washed clothes, warm water was flushed directly into that swamp. Snakes, being cold-blooded, are always looking for warmth, so they were drawn up that drain like a magnet . . . right into the house!

Dawson took appropriate measures to seal off that pipe and create a new drainage system—minus the swamp and snakes. They were all relieved, knowing that the snakes would no longer would be invading.

But the snakes didn't give up so quickly. Mysteriously, they kept showing up around the house, turning the Grover family's relief into grief.

One day Dawson was down in his basement working on a project when he noticed something out of the corner of his eye. A snake was poking its head out from a hole in the wall!

Incredibly, a family of snakes that had come in through the drainpipe (before it was closed off) had made a nest inside the basement wall and was now multiplying!

At last the Grovers had found the final piece to the mystery of the snakes. But they still had to dispose of the intruders. Dawson's son, Peter, banged on the basement wall where the snakes were living. As he did so, the snakes slid out through the hole, escaping (so they thought!) from the frightening sound.

But then they came face-to-face with the head of the house, who was more than glad to terminate the intruders. After the brutal "snakecide" was over, the Grover house was peaceful and safe again.

The most amazing part of this story to me is not the Grovers' battle with the sneaky snakes. It is that the family who lived in the house before them had never bothered to get rid of the varmints! They somehow learned to live with the snakes. That is gross!

What can we learn from the "parable" of the snakes? First, it is essential that we find the way(s) in which Satan, that cruel serpent, has gained access to our lives. Today's Scripture warns us that some people will fall away from the Christian faith. Why? Because they have listened to the hissing whispers of deceitful spirits. They have swallowed his lies—hook, line, and sinker.

As we ask God for discernment, He will expose the areas of sin and compromise in our lives through which the devil has gained control. We close off those avenues of access when we confess and repent (turn away) from our sins and reject (renounce) any lies we have believed.

But there may be nests of snakes in our "walls" as well. Deeply entrenched strongholds of wrong thinking in our lives need to be wiped out too. This happens as we "take every thought captive to the obedience of Christ," reject all lies, and learn the truth of God's Word. Our lives are transformed by the continuous renewing of our minds (Romans 12:2).

Finally, it is possible for Christians to go through their whole lives just *coping* with their sinful struggles—anger, bitterness, lust, fear, worry, and so on—without ever really *conquering* them. This is wrong. Christ has crushed the serpent's head (Genesis 3:15 NIV) so that we can walk in victory over the enemy!

Don't settle for anything less than freedom. Get rid of the snakes in your life today!

Reality Check

Look up the following verses in your Bible. In the blanks provided, summarize what they say about getting rid of the garbage in your life.

Ephesians 4:20-24

1 John 1:5-10

The Lie to Reject

I reject the lie that says the best I can hope for in this life is to cope with the bondage in my life. I refuse to surrender to the enemy's lies that there is no hope of victory over sin in this life.

The Truth to Accept

I accept the truth that I am "more than a conqueror" through Christ who loves me. I recognize that it was for freedom that Christ has set me free so that I can be truly free from my bondage to sin and Satan. Though attacks from the enemy are unavoidable, God's sustaining grace is sufficient to enable me to victoriously endure and overcome all bondage.

Prayer for Today

Dear Lord, I ask You to reveal to me today all the lies from deceitful spirits that I have paid attention to. I don't want to fall away from the faith; I want to fall in love with You. In every case in which the devil has gained a foothold or a stronghold in my life, please show me the path to freedom. I commit myself right now to walking that path, no matter how hard or long it may be. In Jesus' strong name I pray. Amen.

Today's Bible Reading: Titus 1

Further Reading: Acts 5 and 1 Timothy 4

Day 39

The Son Has Won

The reason the Son of God appeared was to destroy the devil's work (1 John 3:8 NIV).

In our daily battles against the world, the flesh, and the devil, one truth needs to ring clear in our hearts and minds:

Jesus is the Victor!

Through His sinless life, perfect sacrifice for sin on the cross, triumphant resurrection from the dead, and glorious ascension to His throne in heaven, Jesus has accomplished what He came to do: destroy the devil's work.

Satan had a stranglehold on the human race through lies, deception, cruel violence, death, and seduction into sinful bondage. Then Jesus came along, and the shackles fell off, the chains were broken, and the prison doors swung wide open. Jesus came to destroy the devil's work. . . . and that's just what He did!

The following testimony comes from a woman we have never met. She attended a Saturday conference which I (Neil) conducted at her church, and she gave this letter to me through her pastor.

Dear Neil,

I have been set free—praise the Lord! Yesterday, for the first time in years, the voices stopped. I could hear the silence. When we sang, I could hear myself sing.

For the first 14 years of my life I lived with an oppressive, abusive mother who never said "I love you" or put her arms around me when I cried. I received no affection, no kind words, no affirmation, no sense of who I was—only physical and emotional abuse. At 15 I was subjected to three weeks of Erhard Seminars Training (now called "The Forum"), which really screwed up my mind. The year which followed was pure hell. My mother threw me out, so I went to live with another family. Eventually they also threw me out.

Three years later I found Christ. My decision to trust Christ was largely based on my fear of Satan and the power of evil I had experienced in my life.

Even though I knew Satan had lost his ownership of me, I was unaware of how vulnerable I still was to his deception and control. For the first two years of my Christian life I was in bondage to a sin I didn't even know was a sin. Once I realized my sin, confessed it to God, and received forgiveness, I thought I was finally free of Satan's attempts to control me. I didn't realize that the battle had only begun.

I suffered from unexplainable rashes, hives, and welts all over my body. I lost my joy and closeness to the Lord. I could no longer sing or quote Scripture. I turned to food as my comfort and security. The demons attacked my sense of right and wrong, and I became involved in immorality in my search for identity and love.

But that all ended yesterday when I renounced Satan's control in my life. I have found the freedom and protection which comes from knowing I am loved. I'm not on a high; I'm writing with a clear mind, a clean spirit, and a calm hand. Even my previous bondage to food seems suddenly foreign to me.

I never realized that a Christian could be so vulnerable to Satan's control. I was deceived, but now I am free. Thank you, thank you, Jesus!

—*Sheila*[1]

A big question that comes up all the time is: Can a Christian be *demon-possessed?* The answer to that question is an absolute no! To be "possessed" means to be "owned." Every believer in Christ is a child of God, bought with the price of the shed blood of the Lord Jesus Christ. He or she belongs to God (1 Corinthians 6:19,20 and 1 Peter 1:17-19).

But can a Christian be influenced, deceived, and even controlled in his attitudes, feelings, and actions by the devil? Absolutely yes! If, for example, you believed Satan's lie that God did not love you anymore because of your sinful behavior, would that affect your life? Of course! Your mind, emotions, and will would be controlled by that view of God. You might give up on the Christian life altogether or you might throw yourself into "religious" activity, hoping to win God's love back again!

But there is no need to lose control to the enemy of your soul. You belong to Jesus Christ, the Son of God. And the Son of God came for this very purpose: to destroy the devil's work... in your life and in mine. Sheila joyfully discovered that the power of Christ was far greater than the deceptions of Satan. That same power is available to you. The Son has won! Believe it today.

Reality Check

Look up the following verses in your Bible. In the blanks provided, summarize what they say about the possibility of demonic control over true believers in God.

Luke 13:10-16

Luke 22:31-14

The Lie to Reject

I reject the lie that I, as a Christian, can be owned by the devil. I also reject the lie that Satan cannot influence or attack me simply because I am a Christian. I recognize both extremes as wrong and unbiblical.

The Truth to Accept

I accept the truth that I belong to God because He purchased me by the blood of the Lord Jesus. I also accept the truth that it is possible for me to fall into deep deception and bondage.

But I announce the truth that Jesus came to destroy the devil's work in my life. Therefore I choose to walk in and rest in the victory of Christ in my life, and to turn away from all evil.

Prayer for Today

Dear heavenly Father, I choose today to be controlled by You and Your Word. Please fill me with the Spirit of truth that I might be guided into all truth. Protect me from the attacks of the enemy by opening my eyes to all of the devil's deceptions designed to control me. I want to reject each and every effort of Satan to lure me into his traps today. I thank You, Lord Jesus, for doing the hard work of destroying the devil's works. May my life be a constant testimony of the victory You won on the cross for me. In Jesus' name. Amen.

Today's Bible Reading: Titus 2

Further Reading: 1 Corinthians 5 and 2 Corinthians 2

Day 40

Keep It Simple

I am afraid, lest as the serpent deceived Eve by his craftiness, your minds should be led astray from the simplicity and purity of devotion to Christ (2 Corinthians 11:3).

Prayer. Prayer meetings. Bible reading. Bible study. Bible memorization. Church worship. Sunday school. Youth group. Retreats. Personal devotions. Giving. Witnessing. Missions.

Sometimes the whole Christian life can seem overwhelming! Who could possibly do it all?

Well, I've got good news for you. You can boil the whole Christian life down to this: *Jesus Christ.*

That's sounds so . . . well, simple, doesn't it? It should, because it's supposed to be.

The Christian life at its purest and simplest is *falling in love with Jesus and trusting Him to guide, protect, and provide for you.* All those things we mentioned in the first paragraph are Christian *activities.* As you grow in your love and trust of *Jesus Christ,* He will guide you into the activities He wants you to be a part of.

An incident from the life of Jesus, found in the Gospel of Luke, illustrates exactly what we're talking about.

> *Now as they were traveling along, He [Jesus] entered a certain village; and a woman named Martha welcomed Him into her home. And she had a sister called Mary, who moreover was listening to the Lord's word, seated at His feet. But Martha was distracted with all her preparations; and she came up to Him and said, "Lord, do You not care that my sister has left me to do all the serving alone? Then tell her to help me." But the Lord answered and said to her, "Martha, Martha, you are worried and bothered about so many things; but only a few things are necessary, really only one, for Mary has chosen the good part, which shall not be taken away from her"* (Luke 10:38-42).

In most households, Martha would have been praised for all her hard work, while Mary would have been viewed as lazy or selfish. But who did Jesus rebuke and who did He commend?

You see, Martha had made her relationship with Jesus too complicated. She probably felt she had to make the house all beautiful, and was busily preparing this wonderful meal for her Lord.

Now there is nothing wrong with serving the Lord. But too often we *serve* Jesus when what God really wants us to do is *seek* Jesus. Mary understood that fact, and Jesus said she had chosen the "good part."

Beware of one of Satan's subtlest deceptions: tricking us into getting so busy with *good* things that we miss the *best* thing of all.

Even doing a 40-day devotional can become just one of many things on our "To-Do List." But that is not the purpose of this book at all. The purpose is to provide some structure for you to spend time with God each day for 40 days. Then, since it takes about six weeks to develop a habit, we hope and pray that you will continue to spend time with God each day as you go through life.

Not because you *have* to, but because you *want* to. There's a world of difference. The first is a relationship of *duty;* the second is a relationship of *love.*

So keep your relationship with God simple. Fix your eyes on Jesus. Get to know Him better. Allow yourself to fall in love with Him, spending unhurried time at His feet. Keep your heart pure—quickly turning away from evil—for the pure in heart shall see God (Matthew 5:8).

And when you find the Christian life becoming a complicated burden and you feel like you are trying to juggle about a dozen spiritual balls in the air, remember Mary. Her sister, Martha, had opened her *home* to Jesus. Mary opened her *heart.*

Reality Check

Look up the following verses in your Bible. In the blanks provided, summarize what they say about our devotion to Jesus.

Luke 17:11-19

John 12:1-8

The Lie to Reject

I reject the lie that the Christian life is complicated and burdensome. I recognize that Satan wants me to get my eyes off Jesus and onto everything else, and I refuse to do that.

The Truth to Accept

I accept the truth that Christ is my life and that my life is hidden with Christ in God. I choose to maintain the simplicity and purity of devotion to Jesus Christ. I make seeking Jesus my priority, knowing that serving Him will flow out of that relationship.

Prayer for Today

Dear heavenly Father, I thank You for reminding me today that my relationship with Jesus comes first. Protect me from all of Satan's tricks to try to complicate and burden my life.

I choose to learn the lesson from the story of Mary and Martha, and I here and now make getting to know Jesus and listening to His Word the number one priority in my life. Even though this 40-day devotional is almost over, I pray that the good habit of daily spending time with You, Lord, will stick. I look forward to many incredible times of being with You, Jesus, in the days and years ahead. And it's in Your name I pray. Amen.

Today's Bible Reading: Titus 3

Further Reading: Psalm 16 and Psalm 73

Notes

Day 4: Face-to-Face with a Murderer

1. Adapted from Nena Benigno, "Sharing the Freedom of Forgiveness," in *People Reaching People* (Philippine Campus Crusade for Christ), vol. XI, no. 1, Sep. 1992, p. 7.
2. Ibid., p. 9.

Day 5: Today Is the Day

1. Charles Colson, *The Body* (Dallas: Word Publishing, 1992), pp. 168-69.

Day 6: Selling Out

1. Neil Anderson and Rich Miller, *Know Light, No Fear* (Nashville: Thomas Nelson Publishers, 1996), p. 69.

Day 11: Hang Tough...Jesus Did!

1. "A changed Seles is set to return to a sport in urgent need of her," in *The Philadelphia Inquirer*, July 25, 1995, p. A18.

Day 16: Prisoners of War

1. Neil Anderson and Dave Park, *The Bondage Breaker, Youth Edition* (Eugene, OR: Harvest House Publishers, 1993), p. 59.

Day 18: The Lyin' Lion

1. Adapted from Neil Anderson and Rich Miller, *Know Light, No Fear* (Nashville: Thomas Nelson Publishers, 1996), p. 53.
2. Neil Anderson and Steve Russo, *The Seduction of Our Children* (Eugene, OR: Harvest House Publishers, 1991), p. 34.

Day 20: A Giant Challenge

1. Adapted from Ronald Combs, "Only a Boy Named David," in *Worldwide Challenge*, January 1982, pp. 14-16.

Day 30: Something's Happening!

1. "Students Lead on Campus," in *The Network News*, Spring 1994, vol. 12, no. 1, p. 1.

Day 31: The Lure of Darkness

1. Neil Anderson, *The Bondage Breaker* (Eugene, OR: Harvest House Publishers, 1993), pp. 118-19.

Day 32: Tailor-Made Temptation

1. Neil Anderson, *The Bondage Breaker* (Eugene, OR: Harvest House Publishers, 1993), pp. 127-28.

Day 35: No Regrets

1. Neil Anderson, *The Bondage Breaker* (Eugene, OR: Harvest House Publishers, 1993), pp. 153-54.

Day 39: The Son Has Won

1. Neil Anderson, *The Bondage Breaker* (Eugene, OR: Harvest House Publishers, 1993), pp. 171-72.

Other Good Harvest House Books for Youth

Awesome God and **Ultimate Love**
by *Neil T. Anderson* and *Rich Miller*

Helping a new generation of teens face the challenges of their world, the devotions in *Awesome God* and *Ultimate Love* focus on God's involvement in day-to-day situations. These two books cover God's plan for love, dating, and relationships.

The Bondage Breaker Youth Edition and
The Bondage Breaker Youth Edition Study Guide
by *Neil T. Anderson* and *Dave Park*
Are you enslaved to negative thoughts, irrational feelings or habitual sin? Do you struggle with sexual temptation, insecurity and fear? In *The Bondage Breaker Youth Edition*, Anderson and Park offer practical help to teens who want to experience true freedom in Christ. *The Bondage Breaker Youth Edition Study Guide* is a clear, exciting and practical approach to implementing the information from the *Bondage Breaker Youth Edition.*

Extreme Faith
by *Neil T. Anderson* and *Dave Park*

"Where do I fit in?" "Where is God when I need Him most?" "Can God use me?" Neil and Dave answer these questions and more as they explore one of the most important truths of the Christian life—a believer's identity in Jesus. These short, challenging devotions offer guidance and direction for finding your way in an increasingly hostile society.

Purity Under Pressure
by *Neil T. Anderson* and *Dave Park*
Do you understand your sexual identity? Few things cause as much confusion and conflict as making the right choices for sexual purity. Have you already started experimenting sexually? Are you desperate to be free of the guilt you carry? In a reassuring style, popular spiritual conflicts counselor Neil Anderson and Freedom in Christ youth director Dave Park will help you grasp the spiritual truths behind the pressures and temptations you face.